Small Ships
Tugs, Freighters, Ferries, & Excursion Boats
Working Vessels and Workboat Heritage Yacht
Designs from the boards of the
Benford Design Group

P.O. Box 447
605 Talbot St.
St. Michaels, MD 21663

Phone: 301-745-3235
Fax: 301-745-9743

Published by:

P.O. Box 447

St. Michaels, MD 21663

Phone: 301-745-3750

Fax: 301-745-9743

Dedication:

To my friend, the late Ron Brown.

He never forgot that these boats had to "look" right in order to be right. I miss the pleasure of working with him and his unflagging optimism.

By the same author:

CRUISING BOATS, SAIL & POWER, 4 editions in 1968, 1969, 1970, & 1971. Catalog of designs and article reprints.

PRACTICAL FERRO-CEMENT BOATBUILD-ING, with Herman Husen, 3 editions in 1970, 1971, and 1972. Best selling construction handbook, a how-to on building in ferro-cement.

DESIGNS & SERVICES, 5 editions, 1971, 1972, 1987, 1988, & 1990. Catalog of plans and services of our firm.

BOATBUILDING & DESIGN FORUM, a monthly newsletter with more information on ferro-cement boatbuilding, 1973.

THE BENFORD 30, 3 editions in 1975, 1976, & 1977. An exposition on the virtues of this design and general philosophy of choosing a cruising boat.

CRUISING DESIGNS, 2 editions in 1975, & 1976. A catalog of plans and services and information about boats & equipment.

CRUISING YACHTS, 1983 hardcover book with a selection of Benford designs covered in detail, including several complete sets of plans and a lot of information about the boats and how they came to be. 8 pages of color photos.

SMALL CRAFT PLANS, 1990 book with 15 sets of full plans for 7'-3" to 18' dinghies and tenders.

SMALL SHIPS, 1990 book with Benford designs for tugs, freighters (like the Florida Bay Coaster), ferries and excursion boats. 10 pages of color photos.

DESIGN DEVELOPMENT OF A 40m SAILING YACHT, Technical paper presented to the Society of Naval Architects & Marine Engineers, at the 5th (1981) Chesapeake Sailing Yacht Symposium, and in the bound transactions of that meeting.

Introduction

I spent my apprentice years (1962 to 1969) working for others, doing a great variety of design work. A significat part of this work involved commercial vessels, and my interest and love for small ships has continued to grow in the ensuing years of running my own design business.

This book is a collection of our working vessel and workboat heritage designs. I find this type to have a refreshing frankness about them, with the absence of tricky styling and glitter and glitz. While too many of the production boats are busy selling sizzle, we've been delivering steak — to those astute enough to recognize the difference.

Some of the designs shown in this book are available as stock boats. Drop us a line or give us a call. We'll be happy to put you in touch with the current builders.

Most of the rest of the plans are ideas — pipe dreams of what might be or ought to be... If one of these appeals to you, let us know and we'll talk about what it would take to turn it into a reality. Or if one suggests a variation, we're always happy to talk about creating a new boat — this is the mainstay of our business.

Jay R. Benford
St. Michaels, Maryland
August 1990

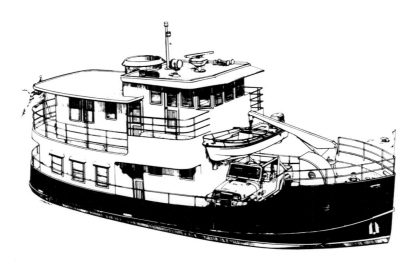

About The Author:

Jay R. Benford was taken sailing before he could walk, by parents unconcerned about the impressions being made on the youth. He was several years old before he determined that this was not perfectly normal procedure on the part of his parents. By then, of course, it was too late for he had become hooked on cruising. His school teachers' pointed remarks about the lack of variety on his book reports (always nautical books) seem to have been of no concern to him. His two years at the University of Michigan led to a much better knowledge of the location of the nautical sections of the libraries than the locations of his classrooms.

He says the best parts of his education were his apprenticeship with John Atkin and the subsequent jobs with a number of boatbuilding firms. After seven years of working for others, he opened his own yacht design office full time in the spring of 1969. Shortly thereafter he got a series of instructive lessons from his accountant in the use of red ink. His recent design work varies from small craft to a 40 meter (131') ketch, and when not off cruising, he can be found in his St. Michaels, MD, office working on one of his dozen or so current design projects.

MORE COMFORTS THAN HOME

Jay Benford's stunning Florida Bay Coaster 65
is a true home away from home.
It even has a space to park the car

STORY BY DOUG HUNTER
PHOTOS BY JIM WILEY

And it came to pass that cruising yachtsmen looking for something solid, proven and reliable in hull design came upon the fishing trawler, and rejoiced greatly, and stuck master staterooms down below where the cod were once piled high on ice. And this enthusiasm for the fishing trawler inspired sane men to cast their eyes about the rest of the commercial fleet. Soon they were leaving dock with their mates and mateys in luxurious comfort, in hulls inspired by lobster boats, and shrimpers, and crabbers, and tugs, and you name it. ▶

The Florida Bay Coaster 65 boasts 1,305 square feet of enclosed living space. Then there's the deck area

With time it seemed the designers had left no port unprobed for fresh inspiration. What could possibly be left for the cruising fraternity to adopt? The dredging barge? The oil rig?

Of course not. But think. Think hard. A kind of boat you have probably been aboard on numerous occasions, probably with the family, and have travelled in comfort from points A to B, the whole time without ever considering what a great yacht this thing would make.

You don't mean —
I do.

* * *

Jay Benford is one of those rare yacht designers whose work is startling and handsome at the same time. There are lots of designers who come up with wild and daring ideas, but too often gimmickry commands the foreground of their vision. Benford's work is firmly anchored in tradition. Sometimes he salutes it with faithful recreations. More often than not he seizes upon the essential elements of the past, tosses in some contemporary yearnings, and whirls the whole thing like a Rubik's cube. You're left with something that makes you think of days gone by even while wondering: why hasn't someone done that before?

On one level Benford is a renovator.

Like someone who buys a handsome brick Victorian home and guts the thing, laying in banks of skylights and open-concept floor plans, Benford seizes on familiar, graceful forms and goes wild within their essential structure. On another level he is a rehabilitator, taking styles of yachts or ships that have either been consigned to the past or deemed unsuitable to the cruising life and making them relevant. More than relevant. Seductively logical.

I defy anyone who loves ships and the sea to peruse Benford's eclectic portfolio and not come across something that makes you feel warm and kind of dizzy, as if you've indulged yourself too long in a hot bath. I am particularly taken by his drawings of the Solarium 44, a plumb-bow fantail motor yacht. Its elliptical aft superstructure surrounds a saloon and galley in a parade of windows which drop open like drawbridges. If you are not overcome by the urge to take this design to the nearest remote anchorage and start lollygagging around in the solarium, then you are without a soul.

The Solarium 44 is typical of Benford's inspirations in that the concept is shot through with evidence of an eye for the essential needs of the good life. This quality is what links the Solarium 44 to the Kanter 64, a rakish pilothouse sloop built by Canada's Kanter Aluminum

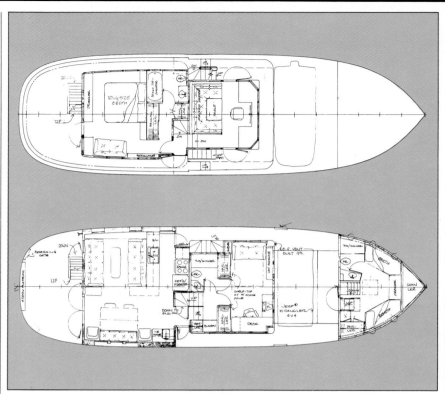

Yachts. And it's what makes them kinfolk of the Florida Bay Coaster 65, the astonishing crowning glory of the Benford pleasure principle.

I don't know anyone who has a thing about ferries the way Benford does. In fact, I don't know anyone other than Benford who has shown a professional interest in making the ferry the cruising yacht of tomorrow. There's nothing in his background, no adolescent signpost, that points to this conviction. He grew up on the south shore of Lake Ontario in Rochester, N.Y. "My folks took me sailing before I could walk," he says. "I've always been cruising." At age 12 he started reading library books on yacht design, and he wound up in the naval architecture program at the University of Michigan.

Benford left one year before completing his degree ("I was too impatient to get to work.") and apprenticed with John Atkin in Connecticut. There followed 18 years as a designer around Puget Sound in the Pacific Northwest — eight of them in Seattle, 10 of them in Friday Harbor. He moved back east, to Maryland, five years ago.

It's out west where you'll find one of Benford's best-known boats, for which he personally is virtually unknown. If you have travelled from Vancouver's downtown waterfront to the shops and restaurants and marine businesses of Granville Island, then you have been a passenger on the Granville Island ferry.

The 20-footer whirls back and forth across False Creek like a diesel-powered waterbug, its passengers snug within the cabin that stretches the length of the boat. The pilot sits dead centre, over the engine; to give him a good view while seated, Benford raised the helm seat and with it the centre of the cabintop in a kind of cupola.

I have a set of blueprints for the ferry. The basic plans were completed Oct. 16, 1983 — by then Benford had relocated to Maryland. But somewhere between that fall day and Feb. 7, 1984, the ferry concept had wormed its way into Benford's imagination, and he had produced a *cruising* version of the False Creek ferry. He gave it a galley, an enclosed head compartment and a settee that converted into a double berth. He called it the Friday Harbor Ferry.

There was no turning back. The concept of the ferry-as-cruiser gave rise to a 34-foot and a 45-foot Friday Harbor Ferry. This served to pique the interest of brothers Reuben and Jerry Trane.

Reuben is the sailor, Jerry the powerboater. About nine years ago Reuben founded the Florida Bay Boat Company and launched a highly idiosyncratic series of coastal cruising sailboats known as Hens. The Mud Hen was the first model, which championed the Reuben Trane philosophy that cruising in any boat under 30 feet was really camping, so let's not kid ourselves. (The Hen moulds were recently sold to Mirage Fibreglass of Palatka, Fla.)

Jerry got Reuben's sights twisted over to powerboats about three years ago when they saw the design for the 45-foot Friday Harbor Ferry. This definitely wasn't camping, but they loved the concept. The aesthetics needed some work, though. What if Benford could bring a tramp-steamer flavour to his ferries-cum-cruisers?

Benford came up with two designs, a 50-footer and a 65-footer, both of which have been built, both of which were on display at the Miami International Boat Show last February. Showgoers were drawn aboard like iron filings to a magnet. There was nothing else even close to them in style or intent.

That intent is to provide luxurious, self-sufficient cruising. Where some powerboats conspire to drag along the comforts of home, Benford's coastal cruiser determines to drag along the whole home. The enclosed-floor-plan space in the 65, which is the subject of the accompanying photographs, is 1,305 square feet. That's bigger than the ground floor of my house, and the ground floor of my house has three bedrooms, a kitchen, a bathroom, a livingroom and a dining room. The conclusion (for me, anyway) is obvious: the 65 has every right to call itself a home. After all, the appliances (which include a washer and dryer and a large freezer) are from Sears. There's even a place to park your car.

Your car in the case of the Coastal Cruiser 65 is a Jeep Wrangler, which rests atop a 10x12-foot cargo bay. The bay is big enough to accommodate a golf cart, and both the Jeep and the cart are moved around with a hydraulic crane mounted on the foredeck. The automobile is a key ingredient in the many Coaster studies Benford has developed. Even the smallest version, a 40-footer, can accommodate a Suzuki Samurai.

The tall superstructure and the sight of a Jeep on deck give the Coastal

CONTINUED ON PAGE 15

The master cabin in the 65
is a masterpiece of air and light.
From the outside, the 50
and 65 (right) demonstrate
their tramp- steamer/ferry heritage

Reprinted courtesy of
MOTOR BOATING & SAILING

Take Her Anywhere

From a mangrove swamp in the Keys to a dock
in Rio, this 65-foot, steel-hulled Coaster,
with a Jeep on one deck and a hot tub on another,
will take you anywhere you want to go.

Story by PETER A. JANSSEN
Photos by ERIC SCHWEIKARDT

The setting could have been scripted by Joseph Conrad, Ernest Hemingway, or Mark Twain—the towering, three-story, steel-hulled 65-foot "personal freighter" gracefully working her way through the mangrove swamps of the Florida Keys, edging through cuts only a few feet wider than her beam, occasionally backing and filling, carving a slalom course in reverse as she nimbly negotiated bends in the stream.

One of the great head-turners of all time, the Florida Bay Coaster 65 drew crowds wherever she went. Fishermen in tiny skiffs putted across the mangrove swamps to get a good look in the Keys; lines formed at the dock at the Mi-ami International Boat Show. This particular vessel, aptly called the *Key Largo*, even attracted a small crowd (actually, just about everybody in the neighborhood) when she pulled into Al-abama Jack's on a little two-lane road just north of—Key Largo. On the other hand, you have to admit it's not hard to attract a crowd when a green-hulled 65-foot boat pulls up, swings a crane from the well deck and first unloads a 17-foot Mako into the water as a dink, and then proceeds to unload a full-sized Jeep onto the beach (just in case you might want to send out a shoreside scouting party). As I said, the Florida Bay Coast-er does draw a crowd.

She also draws about the greatest amount of audible admiration I've ever *On the Florida Bay Coaster 65, the transom folds down, becoming a swim platform or launching area, and a crane on the well deck swings a Mako and a Jeep off the boat.*

encountered aboard a new boat. The quantity of ooohs and aaahs absolutely went off the scale. Most people, when they first see the Coaster, start to grin. It's that kind of a boat. The fact that she holds about 30 people without crowd-ing, and that a good five or six of them are in the top-deck hot tub at any given time, leads to more grins—and then questions about how the grinner can buy one.

This is a boat that appeals to every-body (everybody, that is, who can think

of parting with $600,000 for the basic boat and about $750,000 for one like the *Key Largo* with all the goodies). But there is no doubt that the Coaster has enormous universal appeal. If you want to party, there's room on three decks, with wide-open aft "patios" on the first two decks and then the entire sunning, lounging and hot tubbing area on top. The top deck also has the mandatory ice maker and wet bar.

On the other hand, if you want privacy, the boat is set up to be run by two; it's hard to imagine a more romantic, getaway-from-it-all vessel than the go-anywhere Coaster. If you want to cruise with family or friends, there's an entirely separate cabin forward—in front of the "well deck" with the Jeep and the

Mako—with two beds (not berths) and its own full-sized bathroom (not head). (All the interior space on the Coaster really is big enough to qualify for house-style designations, not the more-diminishing nautical terms.) If you want to live aboard, this is the boat to do it on; you have a living room, enormous bedroom of your own (with its own bath), a guest bedroom (or study), also with its own bath, and then the forward bedroom. In addition to a regular kitchen, there's also a washer and dryer and storage areas in the basement (a/k/a the hold).

The Coaster is indeed a boat with elbow room, lots of elbow room. I was on board for about an hour before I realized that there were half a dozen other peo-

Clockwise from top left: The enormous main salon; an aerial view of the hot tub on the sun deck; the pilothouse; and looking up from the master bedroom.

ple—friends of the owner's nephew who were all on spring break from Duke—on board too.

The Coaster is the brainchild of Reuben Trane, founder, president and chief engineer of the Florida Bay Boat Co. in Miami. He started the company ten years ago, to build the small Mud Hen sailboats, when he got tired of his first career as a movie producer.

A tall, tanned, good-looking guy with a salt and pepper mustache, Trane launched his movie career by winning a mini-Academy Award for the 20-minute "Manhattan Melody" he produced for his master's thesis at Columbia University. "That," he says now, "was the best movie I ever made."

After that, he moved on to flash and trash epics including "King Frat," which even he describes as "a rip-off of 'Animal House'" and "Shockwave," which he says "was about Nazi zombies who live under water. To get enough extras we put ads in the paper saying we wanted zombies for a horror movie. You should have seen the people who answered that one." In the end, Trane ended up having fun, but he also was making movies "that I didn't want my family to see."

A boating enthusiast all his life, Trane changed from making celluloid images to making fiberglass sailboats. After that ran its course, he looked around for other things to do—and the Florida Bay Coasters were born. Basically, Trane created a boat that he wanted himself, one with a slice of the market all to itself. (After all, no matter how successful he is, he isn't going to be churning out thousands of Florida Bay Coasters every year.) "I figured that if I liked the boat, there would be enough other people who liked it too, so that we could have a profitable business," he says.

Room To Spare

So two years ago Trane hooked up with Jay Benford, a naval architect from St. Michael's, Md., and basically asked him to design a big personal freighter, something like an old tramp steamer, a displacement vessel that could hold enough stores, water and fuel to stay away from a dock as long as the owner wanted to stay away from a dock.

Benford fired up his drawing board and produced the Coaster series, first a 50-footer, weighing in at 90,000 pounds, then the 65-footer, at 150,000 pounds, and, coming soon, a 45-footer. They're all built with an all-steel hull, to commercial ship standards, and the exteriors look almost like tramp steamers. Each is fitted with a foredeck crane to load the skiff and Jeep on and off the boat, and they all come with an enormous hold below the well deck, plus a spacious—and extremely comfortable—pilothouse two levels above the main deck to give a commanding view of the water.

And they have lots of room. The master suite of the 65-foot *Key Largo*, for example, has a kingsize bed with more walkaround space than is available in most master bedrooms. (It also has a ceiling fan, reminiscent of Rick's saloon in "Casablanca," and then a 5-by-8-foot skylight. The main salon, utilizing the boat's entire 20-foot beam, looks like a living room at home—except that all the side windows, and the big glass doors leading to the aft "patio" deck, overlook the water. "She's as homelike as possible," says Gerry Trane, Reuben's brother, who is vice president of the company. "Our vessels are meant to be used as either a primary or secondary waterfront home."

The *Key Largo* is a comfortable home, at that, with hardwood oak flooring, pickled oak cabinetry and doors, full-size tile baths in all three staterooms, a leather-appointed study (a/k/a the guest stateroom), plus an air-conditioned "laundry room" in the hold with a 15-cubic-foot deep freeze—and the six-person spa on the sun deck.

A Go-Anywhere Vessel

If all this is almost, but not exactly, what you have in mind, Reuben Trane will change it. "By offering the boater a viable alternative to production boats, we have found ourselves in a unique niche in the marketplace," he says. But if you want something in a slightly different niche, Trane is only too happy to oblige. "We'll give the customer exactly what he or she wants in a displacement cruiser," he says. "By using ship-building techniques, we provide an easily maintained, 'go-anywhere vessel' on the outside with whatever interior spaces and styling are desired on the inside."

One of the nicest spots inside the *Key Largo* is the pilothouse, truly one of the most pleasant I've ever been in. At the back is a big U-shaped leather sofa surrounding a huge high/low table. At the front is a 36-inch stainless destroyer-type wheel, a Wagner compass and rudder angle indicator, one-mile spotlight (the bulb costs $90), and all the normal electronics for long-range cruising. Visibility is excellent with eight windows in front and two on each side. Two doors on each side of the full-width house open to port and starboard wings for observation and docking. There are separate control stations on each side. With the station in the pilothouse, plus the one on the top sun deck, the captain can

choose from among four permanent vantage points—plus there's a portable control station that plugs into several additional positions all around the boat.

The *Key Largo*, despite its size and heft, proved to be extremely maneuverable, swinging easily in her own length. With the help of the optional 25-hp Wesmar bow thruster, you can even parallel park. Twin Cat 3208T diesels, providing 320 hp each, power 3:1 Twin Disc gears; they're hooked up to 2.5-inch stainless shafts driving 32-inch bronze four-blade props. A Kohler 20 kW generator is standard; the *Key Largo* has two. The props are widely spaced, giving the boat its maneuverability; they're also protected by unique strut extensions that drop below the props, and then run back under the rudders in case you bounce off the bottom in some remote part of the world.

1,643-Mile Range

The Coaster cruises at 9.2 knots at 2100 rpm, burning 14 gallons of fuel an hour. Fuel capacity is an enormous 2,500 gallons. In case you want to stay put, the transom has an enormous folding gate that swings down so you can get the Sunfish, windsurfers and jet skis that have been stored in the hold into the water. And when you're ready to weigh anchor, the Ideal 120 v.a.c. reversible capstan does all the work.

All this isn't bad for a company that was making only small, no-nonsense sailboats just two years ago. And Reuben Trane is looking ahead. He can build six Coasters this year, he says, and next year the capacity will double.

He's also a man who is happy in his work. Maneuvering the *Key Largo* through the mangrove swamps, avoiding the skiffs and fishermen who have come over to take a look, he says, "The best thing is that there's no work involved in having this boat. I like the idea where the boat works for you—and you don't work for the boat." ⚓

FLORIDA BAY COASTER 65

LOA	65'
LWL	64'6"
Beam	20'
Draft	4'6"
Disp	150,000 lbs.
Water	1,250 gals.
Fuel	2,500 gals.
Power	Twin Cat 3208Ts

CONTINUED FROM PAGE 9

Cruiser a top-heavy appearance, yet the design is quite stable. The hull form and generous beam give the boat more stability than a lot of conventional motor yachts. Nor is the 65 as ponderous as I had imagined. While we weren't able to leave the dock, Benford says that the 65 cruises at 10 to 10.5 knots, and achieves hull speed at only three-quarter rpm, thanks to the pair of Caterpillar 3208TAs tucked into their own walk-in engine rooms. The Cats are so up to the job that the 65 can reach its cruising speed on one engine alone. Each engine room also houses a 20-kw Kohler generator built on a Yanmar diesel block. Up top, controls for the engines and bow thruster are located outboard as well as on the bridge (which is equipped with commercial ship windows and a rotating clear-view screen), and there's an MMC remote forward.

As pretty as this vessel is inside, it means business. The 65 is built to American Bureau of Shipping standards for small steel ships up to 200 feet in length. The hull is ¼-inch thick, with 3/16ths plate used on the lower works and ⅛-inch on the upper works. Four watertight doors divide the belowdecks into six compartments; framing is both transverse and longitudinal. Beneath the aft deck is a hold area large enough to house a proper scuba diving shop. A compressor allows you to run air-powered tools anywhere on the boat.

Such attention to detail does not come cheap. The base price of the 65 is US$595,000. Fully equipped, it goes for US$750,000. I don't know if that includes the Jeep. At three-quarters of a million bucks all up, I don't think the Jeep's status as an option is that important.

Not many Canadians are in a position to acquire one of these fine craft. They're certainly in a position to appreciate one. About a year ago Wye Heritage Marina in Midland, Ont., sounded out its clientele on their interest in a possible new breed of cruiser suited to poking around Georgian Bay. The marina, which has metal fabricating capability, included a drawing in its newsletter designed to stimulate brainstorming. The drawing was of a Florida Bay Coaster.

I lounged around with Benford for a while in the main living area of the 65.

There aren't many boats that I could truly live aboard. This was one of them, perhaps the only one. Living aboard invariably means compromise. Not on this boat. There were plenty of walls for paintings, a nice office area forward, hard-wearing oak floors, and no weird storage areas in the kitchen (definitely not a galley) propagated by curving topsides. I confessed to Benford that the only drawback I could find was a lack of room for my piano, a cabinet grand.

No problem. "Take out the wet bar," said Benford, pointing to a feature on the starboard side that was clearly superfluous, given its proximity to the upright fridge-freezer in the kitchen. Besides, he had a 55 in the works with a piano.

But if you own a Donzi 16 runabout, a Lamborghini 4x4, a mini-sub and a Hughes 500 helicopter, nothing less than the 100-foot Florida Bay Coaster will do. Benford has drawn only an outboard profile for that model. If you own more than a piano — say a string quartet — I'm sure he could squeeze it in. ⚓

Doug Hunter is the editor of CY

Solarium 44

This 44' Fantail Motor Yacht has a wonderful and airy glassed in cabin in the stern, from whence her name. These can be screened and opened to provide great year-round living. The rest of the accommodations provide for a roomy liveaboard.

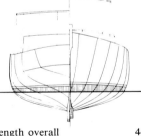

Length overall	44'-0"
Length designed waterline	40'-0"
Beam	12'-0"
Draft	3'-0"
Freeboard:	
Forward	6'-0¾"
Least	3'-9¾"
Aft	4'-9¼"
Displacement, cruising trim	20,950
Displacement-length ratio	146
Prismatic coefficient	.549
Pounds per inch immersion	1,450
Entrance half-angle	19⁰
Water tankage	200 Gals.
Fuel tankage	250 Gals.
Headroom	6'-5"

Gene Coan Photo

Part 2 — Tug Designs

Early in my career in yacht design I spent a couple years (1966 to 1968) as the staff naval architect for Foss Launch & Tug in Seattle. As I recall, at the time Foss operated about a hundred tugs and a couple hundred barges doing all sorts of services. I was fortunate to be part of the design and creation of several tugs while with them, from small harbor tugs to larger, ocean going tugs. The row of silhouettes at the bottom of this page are from the tugs designed during my time with Foss.

Since that time, I've had the opportunity to put this experience with real working tugs to good use, creating a number of others, both for work and pleasure. As will be seen in the following section of this book, I've continued to enjoy looking at and creating new tugs.

Many of the more recent tug designs we've done have been tug yachts, with modest power for economical cruising and more spacious accommodations than would be found aboard a working vessel.

Most of the tug yachts can be powered to do useful work, whether as a harbor tug, yarding boats around for service work, or towing equipment for diving, salvage, or repair work.

The MARTHA FOSS, shown in the above photo is 80' long and has a 27' beam. She is a single screw, powered with a D399 Caterpillar diesel driving an 88 inch diameter propellor. This prop operates in a steering Kort nozzle, with very close tip clearance. This provides the thrust equal to a much larger powerplant. She's proven an excellent worker, doing log towing, ship handling, and general towing work.

14' Tug

This 14-footer makes a splendid harbor and yard tug. She's great for small towing jobs and for moving larger boats around for service and haulouts. She only needs between five and ten horsepower to move her, and the balance of any power installed would be for doing work. The engine we've shown on the plans is the 50 horsepower Yanmar diesel. It won't drive her any faster, for she has a true displacement hull form, but it will make working easier with the thrust from the large diameter prop and the 3.3:1 reduction gear.

If the roomy trawler yacht version isn't enough space for your cruising, how about building a home afloat on a barge? It could be moved around with the little tug when you wanted to relocate or just go for a cruise. Then, you would still have the little tug for trips to town for shopping or doing little work projects to earn more money for the cruising fund.

You could tow a barge for diving and salvage work. Or you could have a floating workshop that you moved to the site of the next project. The possibilities are limited only by your imagination...

The preliminary drawing shown here is an idea of a steel version. We sketched this up while considering an alternative to carrying the 4x4 on the freighter KEY LARGO. This sort of hull form would also be easily done in aluminum or plywood.

Gene Coan's GRIVIT (above) and Jim Lesovsky's FANNY PRATT are sisterships, built to the Tug-Cruiser version of the 14' Tug plans. Photos courtesy of the owners.

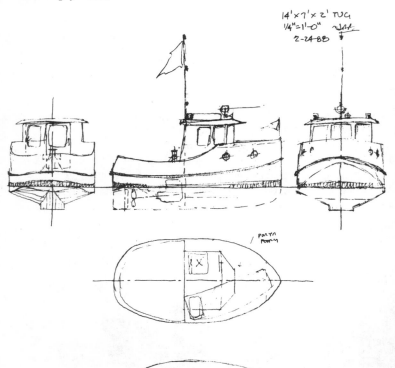

14' x 7' x 2' TUG
1/4" = 1'-0"
2-24-88

Two of the tug versions are shown above. Clarence Butz's BULLHEAD is above left and Joe Failing's 14-footer is rafted alongside the bigger working tug.

Below is Gene Coan's GRIVIT on her mooring on Lake Washington looking the personification of a small ship. Photos courtesy of the owners.

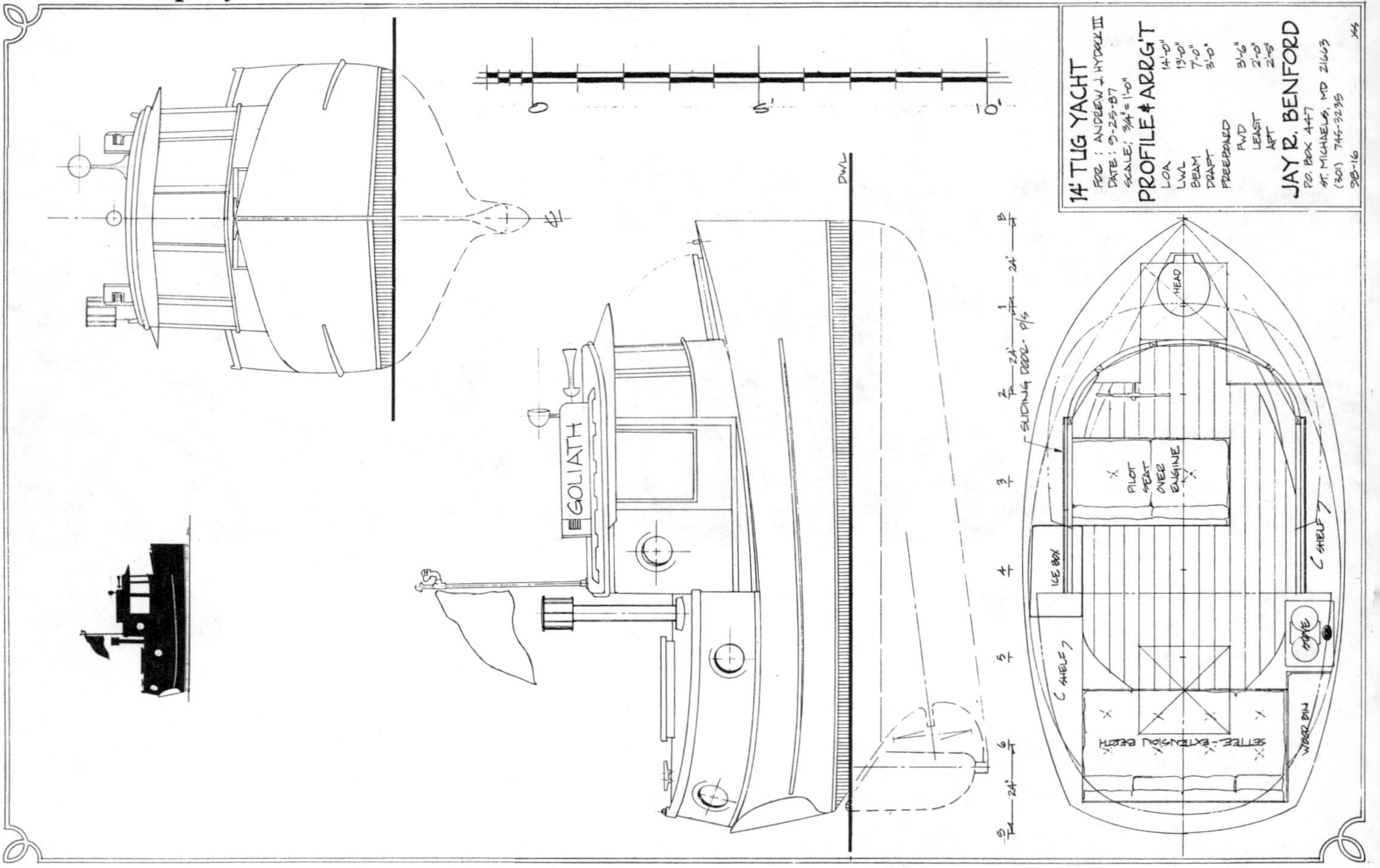

14' TUG YACHT
FOR : ANDREW J. HYDRO III
DATE : 9-25-87
SCALE : 3/4" = 1'-0"

LOA	14'-0"	
LWL	13'-0"	
BEAM	7'-0"	
DRAFT	3'-0"	
FREEBOARD :	FWD	3'6"
	LEAST	2'0"
	AFT	2'6"

PROFILE & ARR'G'T.

JAY R. BENFORD
P.O. BOX 447
ST. MICHAELS, MD 21663
(301) 745-3235
98-16

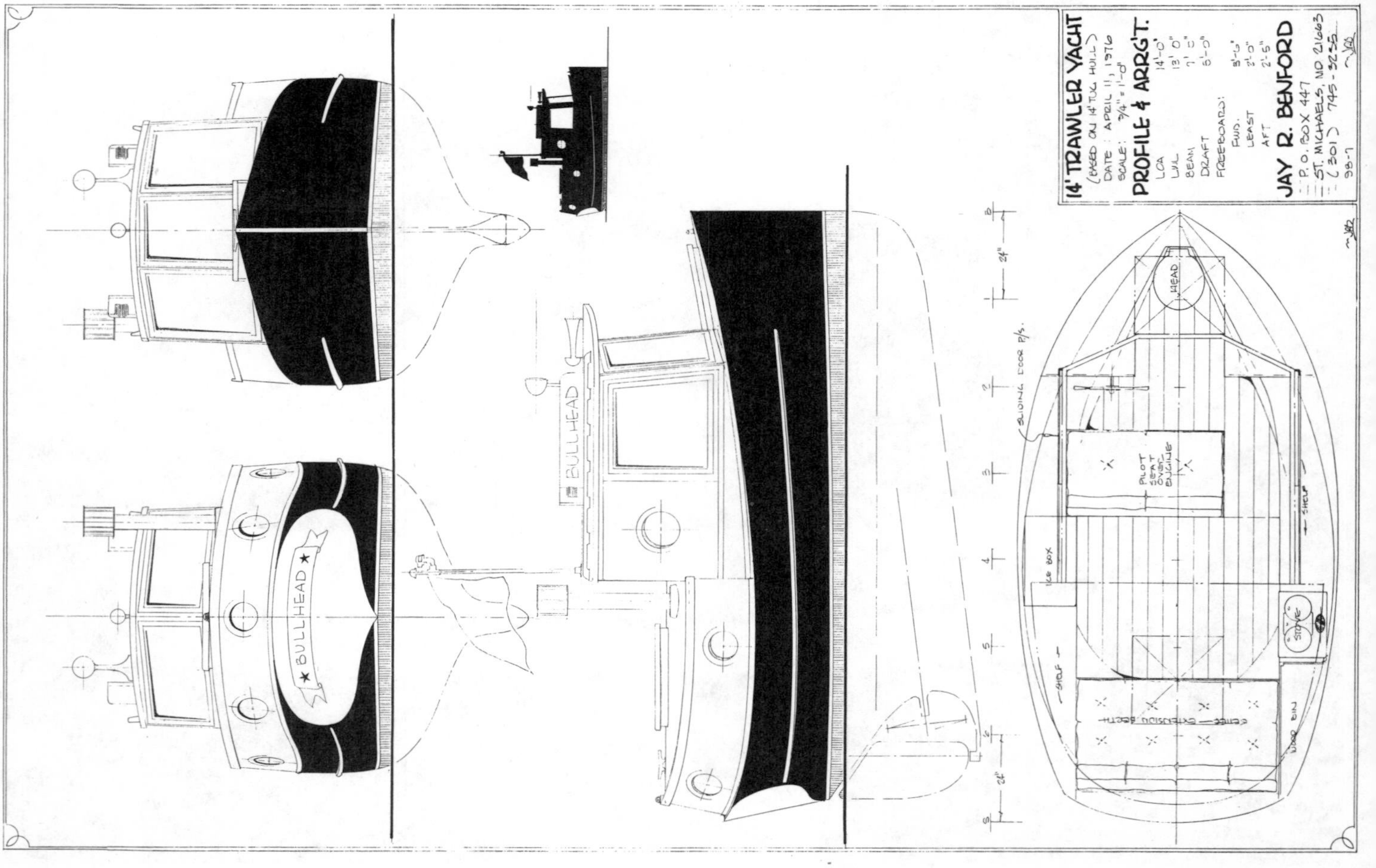

14' TRAWLER YACHT
(BASED ON 14' TUG HULL)
DATE : APRIL 11, 1976
SCALE : 3/4" = 1'-0"

LOA	14'-0"	
LWL	13'-0"	
BEAM	7'-0"	
DRAFT	3'-0"	
FREEBOARD :	FWD	3'6"
	LEAST	2'0"
	AFT	2'6"

PROFILE & ARR'G'T.

JAY R. BENFORD
P.O. BOX 447
ST. MICHAELS, MD 21663
(301) 745-3235
98-1

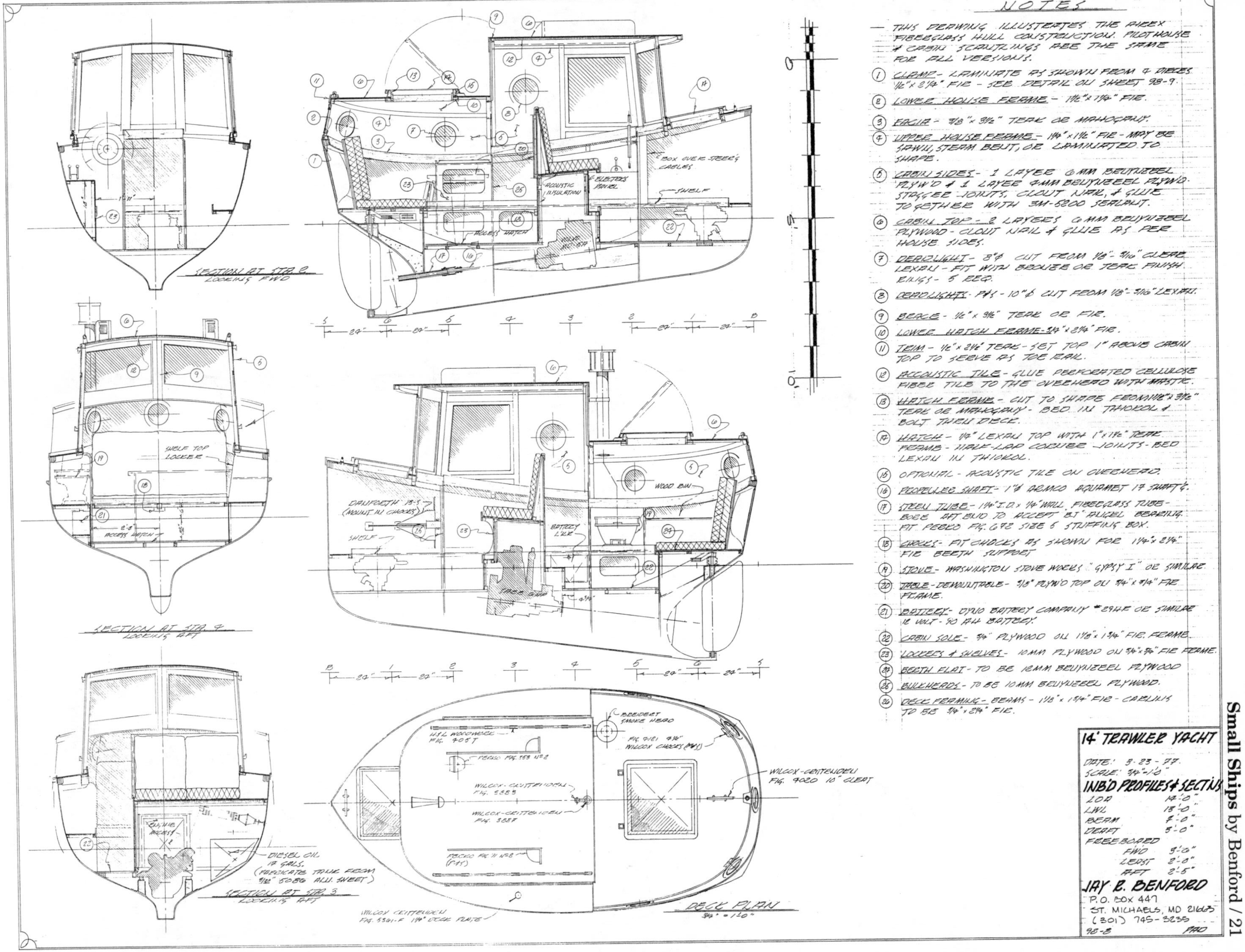

NOTES
— THIS DRAWING ILLUSTRATES THE AIREX FIBERGLASS HULL CONSTRUCTION. PILOTHOUSE & CABIN SCANTLINGS ARE THE SAME FOR ALL VERSIONS.
① CLAMP - LAMINATE AS SHOWN FROM 4 PIECES 1/2"x 2 1/4" FIR - SEE DETAIL ON SHEET 98-9.
② LOWER HOUSE FRAME - 1 1/2" x 1 3/4" FIR.
③ FACIA - 3/8" x 3 1/2" TEAK OR MAHOGANY.
④ UPPER HOUSE FRAME - 1 1/4" x 1 1/2" FIR - MAY BE SAWN, STEAM BENT, OR LAMINATED TO SHAPE.
⑤ CABIN SIDES - 1 LAYER 6MM BRUYNZEEL PLYW'D & 1 LAYER 4MM BRUYNZEEL PLYW'D. STAGGER JOINTS, CLOUT NAIL, & GLUE TOGETHER WITH 3M-5200 SEALANT.
⑥ CABIN TOP - 2 LAYERS 6MM BRUYNZEEL PLYWOOD - CLOUT NAIL & GLUE AS PER HOUSE SIDES.
⑦ DEADLIGHT - 8"∅ CUT FROM 1/8" - 3/16" CLEAR LEXAN - FIT WITH BRONZE OR TEAK FINISH RINGS - 5 REQ.
⑧ DEADLIGHTS - P&S - 10"∅ CUT FROM 1/8" - 3/16" LEXAN.
⑨ BRACE - 1/2" x 3 1/2" TEAK OR FIR.
⑩ LOWER HATCH FRAME - 3/4" x 2 1/4" FIR.
⑪ TRIM - 1/2" x 2 1/2" TEAK - SET TOP 1" ABOVE CABIN TOP TO SERVE AS TOE RAIL.
⑫ ACOUSTIC TILE - GLUE PERFORATED CELLULOSE FIBER TILE TO THE OVERHEAD WITH MASTIC.
⑬ HATCH FRAME - CUT TO SHAPE FROM 1 1/2" x 3 1/2" TEAK OR MAHOGANY - BED IN THIOKOL & BOLT THRU DECK.
⑭ HATCH - 1/4" LEXAN TOP WITH 1" x 1 1/2" TEAK FRAME - HALF-LAP CORNER JOINTS - BED LEXAN IN THIOKOL.
⑮ OPTIONAL - ACOUSTIC TILE ON OVERHEAD.
⑯ PROPELLER SHAFT - 1"∅ ARMCO AQUAMET 17 SHAFT'G.
⑰ STERN TUBE - 1 1/4" I.D. x 1/4" WALL FIBERGLASS TUBE - BORE AFT END TO ACCEPT "BJ" RUBBER BEARING. FIT PERKO FIG. 672 SIZE 5 STUFFING BOX.
⑱ CHOCKS - FIT CHOCKS AS SHOWN FOR 1 1/4" x 2 1/4" FIR BERTH SUPPORT.
⑲ STOVE - WASHINGTON STOVE WORKS "GYPSY I" OR SIMILAR.
⑳ TABLE - DEMOUNTABLE - 3/8" PLYW'D TOP ON 3/4" x 3/4" FIR FRAME.
㉑ BATTERY - DYNO BATTERY COMPANY #29HR OR SIMILAR 12 VOLT - 90 AH BATTERY.
㉒ CABIN SOLE - 3/4" PLYWOOD ON 1 1/8" x 1 3/4" FIR FRAME.
㉓ LOCKERS & SHELVES - 10MM PLYWOOD ON 3/4" x 3/4" FIR FRAME.
㉔ BERTH FLAT - TO BE 12MM BRUYNZEEL PLYWOOD.
㉕ BULKHEADS - TO BE 10MM BRUYNZEEL PLYWOOD.
㉖ DECK FRAMING - BEAMS - 1 1/8" x 1 3/4" FIR - CARLINS TO BE 3/4" x 2 1/4" FIR.
14' TRAWLER YACHT
DATE: 3-23-77
SCALE: 3/4" = 1'0"
INB'D PROFILES & SECT'NS
LOA 14'0"
LWL 13'0"
BEAM 7'0"
DRAFT 3'0"
FREEBOARD
FWD 3'0"
LEAST 2'0"
AFT 2'5"
JAY R. BENFORD
P.O. BOX 447
ST. MICHAELS, MD 21663
(301) 745-3235
98-8
0
5'
10'
SECTION AT STA. 2
LOOKING FWD
SECTION AT STA. 4
LOOKING AFT
SECTION AT STA. 3
LOOKING AFT
DECK PLAN
3/4" = 1'0"
BOX OVER STEER'G CABLES
SHELF
ACOUSTIC INSULATION
ELECTRICS PANEL
ACCESS HATCH
SHELF TOP LOCKER
ACCESS HATCH
DANFORTH 13-S (MOUNT IN CHOCKS)
SHELF
BATTERY LKR
WOOD BIN
ENGINE ACCESS
DIESEL OIL 17 GALS. (FABRICATE TANK FROM 3/32" 5086 ALU. SHEET)
BREIDERT SMOKE HEAD
H.I.L. WOODWORK FIG. 405T
PERKO FIG. 553 Nº2
FIG. 9181 4 1/2" WILCOX CHOCKS (P&S)
WILCOX-CRITTENDEN FIG. 4020 10" CLEAT
WILCOX-CRITTENDEN FIG. 5585
WILCOX-CRITTENDEN FIG. 3887
PERKO FIG. 11 Nº8 (P&S)
WILCOX CRITTENDEN FIG. 5341-F 1 1/4" DECK PLATE

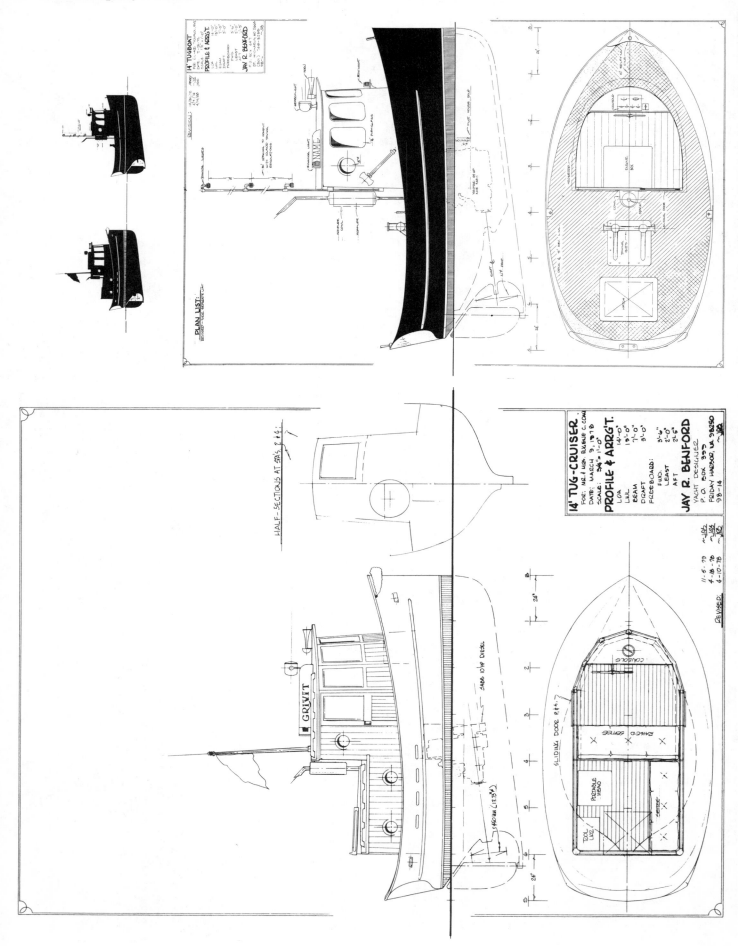

20' Tug

This 20' tug has the classic working tug's fantail stern, giving her a very graceful appearance. This hull shape also lets her slip through the water at modest speeds with very modest fuel consumption.

Like all our tug designs, the pilothouse has standing headroom. She has space for a couple of adults to cruise aboard in comfort. Her cockpit is a nice place to sit and watch the scenery slide by, and it would be easy to rig an awning over the after half of the boat for shade and shelter.

It would be straightforward to set up a second steering station in the cockpit, like the one on BATEN, the 20' supply boat shown next in the book. This is sometimes handy to have when making singlehanded landings and for operating on those days when the weather is just right.

She could also be done as a harbor launch for carrying groups of people to and from their boats. The little ferries shown later in this book are very capable at this service too.

Molded fiberglass hulls are available from a mold located in Portland, Oregon, for those wanting a head start on building one of these little ships.

The 20-footer above is one of the first of the fiberglass hulled versions of this design. We met up with her on a cruise to Bellingham, Washington.

The sistership below was cold-molded by George Koran and LOGE cruises on the Chesapeake Bay. Photos courtesy of the owner.

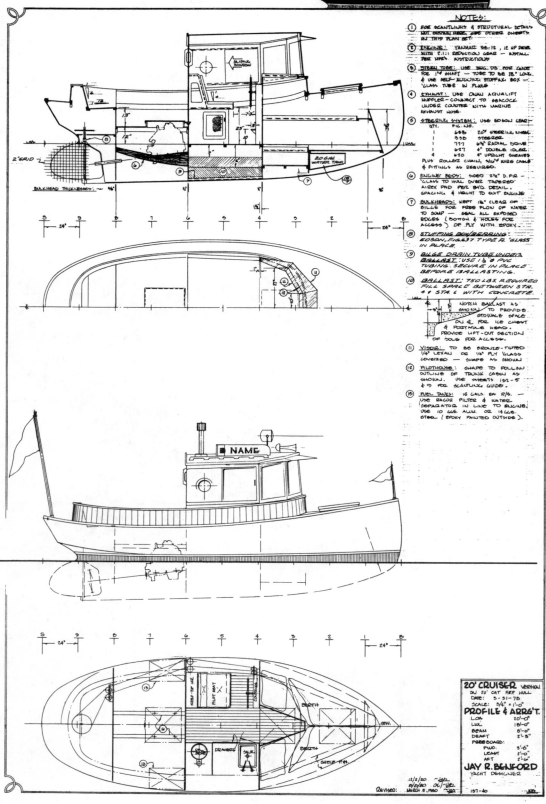

NOTES:

① FOR SCANTLINGS & STRUCTURAL DETAILS NOT SHOWN HERE, SEE OTHER SHEETS IN THIS PLAN SET.

② ENGINE: YANMAR 3G-12, 12 HP DSL. WITH 2.21:1 REDUCTION GEAR — INSTALL PER MFRS. INSTRUCTIONS.

③ STERN TUBE: USE BRG. DB FOR CORE FOR 1" SHAFT — TUBE TO BE 18" LONG & USE SELF-ALIGNING STUFFING BOX — 'GLASS TUBE IN PLACE.

④ EXHAUST: USE ONAN AQUALIFT MUFFLER — CONNECT TO SEACOCK UNDER COUNTER WITH MARINE EXHAUST HOSE.

⑤ STEERING SYSTEM: USE EDSON GEAR.
QTY. FIG. NO.
1   68B   20" STEERING WHEEL
1   55D   STEERER
1   777   6½" RADIAL DRIVE
4   637   6" DOUBLE IDLER
4   620   4" UPRIGHT SHEAVES
PLUS ROLLER CHAIN, 3/16" WIRE CABLE & FITTINGS AS REQUIRED.

⑥ ENGINE BEDS: SIDES 2½" D. FIR — 'GLASS TO HULL OVER TAPERED AIREX PAD PER BHD DETAIL. SPACING & HEIGHT TO SUIT ENGINE.

⑦ BULKHEADS: KEPT 1½" CLEAR OF BILGE FOR FREE FLOW OF WATER TO SUMP — SEAL ALL EXPOSED EDGES (BOTTOM & HOLES FOR ACCESS) OF PLY WITH EPOXY.

⑧ STUFFING BOX/BEARING: EDSON, FIG 637 TYPE A. 'GLASS IN PLACE.

⑨ BILGE DRAIN TUBE UNDER BALLAST: USE 1½" Ø PVC TUBING. SECURE IN PLACE BEFORE BALLASTING.

⑩ BALLAST: 750 LBS. REQUIRED FILL SPACE BETWEEN STA. 4 & STA. 6 WITH CONCRETE.

NOTCH BALLAST AS SHOWN TO PROVIDE STOWAGE SPACE ON ℄ FOR ICE CHEST & PORTABLE HEAD. PROVIDE LIFT-OUT SECTION OF SOLE FOR ACCESS.

⑪ VISOR: TO BE BRONZE-TINTED ¼" LEXAN OR ¼" PLY 'GLASS COVERED — SHAPE AS SHOWN.

⑫ PILOTHOUSE: SHAPE TO FOLLOW OUTLINE OF TRUNK CABIN AS SHOWN. USE SHEETS 152-5 & 9 FOR SCANTLING GUIDE.

⑬ FUEL TANKS: 15 GALS. EA. P/S. — USE RACOR FILTER & WATER SEPARATOR IN LINE TO ENGINE. USE 10 GA. ALUM. OR 14 GA. STEEL (EPOXY PAINTED OUTSIDE).

20' CRUISER VERSION
ON 20' CAT. KER HULL
DATE: 3-31-78
SCALE: 3/4" = 1'-0"
PROFILE & ARR'G'T.

LOA   20'-0"
LWL   18'-0"
BEAM   8'-0"
DRAFT   2'-5"
FREEBOARD:
  FWD.   3'-6"
  LEAST   2'-0"
  AFT   2'-6"

JAY R. BENFORD
YACHT DESIGNER

REVISED: 12/2/80, 8/2/80, 06/3/82, MARCH 5, 1980   157-40

20' Supply Boat BÅTEN

BÅTEN was designed to be the supply boat and pickup truck for two friends living on a small island that was without ferry service. They needed a dependable boat to get them back and forth to the larger island nearby in whatever the weather was, 365 days a year.

In service for over a decade, she's proven herself very capable, carrying hundreds of passengers. She's also carried a variety of cargoes, from groceries to the materials to build a barn.

The longer cabin cruiser version is suited for areas that need either a heated or air-conditioned cabin. The big windows on the sides and aft end should be arranged to slide, so they function as doors for entry and exit.

BATEN picking up a load of barn materials at Friday Harbor. They were moved five miles to Crane Island, one of many uses for this marine pickup truck.

BATEN leaving Friday Harbor after her crew and the designer had a pleasant lunch at one of the several restaurants overlooking the harbor. The wood stove in her pilothouse makes it pleasant aboard during the cooler months.

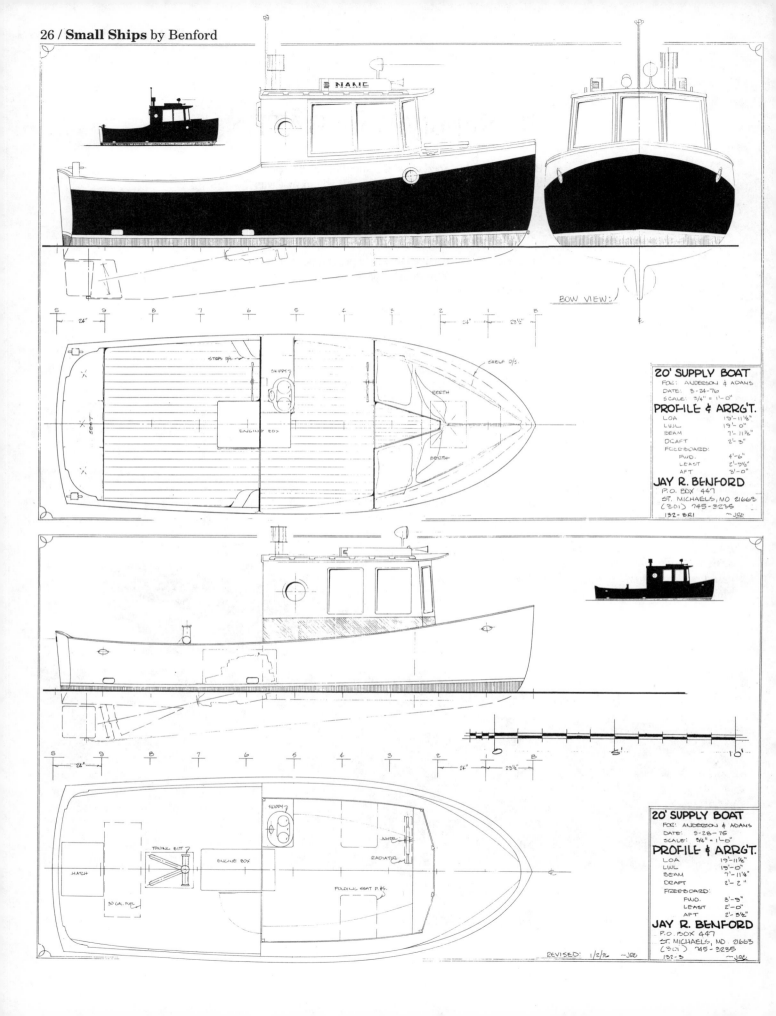

BOW VIEW

20' SUPPLY BOAT
FOR: ANDERSON & ADAMS
DATE: 3-24-76
SCALE: 3/4" = 1'-0"
PROFILE & ARRG'T.
LOA	19'-11½"
LWL	19'-0"
BEAM	7'-11½"
DRAFT	2'-3"
FREEBOARD:	
FWD.	4'-6"
LEAST	2'-5½"
AFT	3'-0"

JAY R. BENFORD
P.O. BOX 447
ST. MICHAELS, MD 21663
(301) 745-3235
132-BRI   ~JRB

20' SUPPLY BOAT
FOR: ANDERSON & ADAMS
DATE: 9-28-76
SCALE: 3/4" = 1'-0"
PROFILE & ARRG'T.
LOA	19'-11½"
LWL	19'-0"
BEAM	7'-11½"
DRAFT	2'-2"
FREEBOARD:	
FWD.	3'-8"
LEAST	2'-0"
AFT	2'-5½"

JAY R. BENFORD
P.O. BOX 447
ST. MICHAELS, MD 21663
(301) 745-3235
132-B   ~JRB

REVISED: 1/2/76 ~JRB

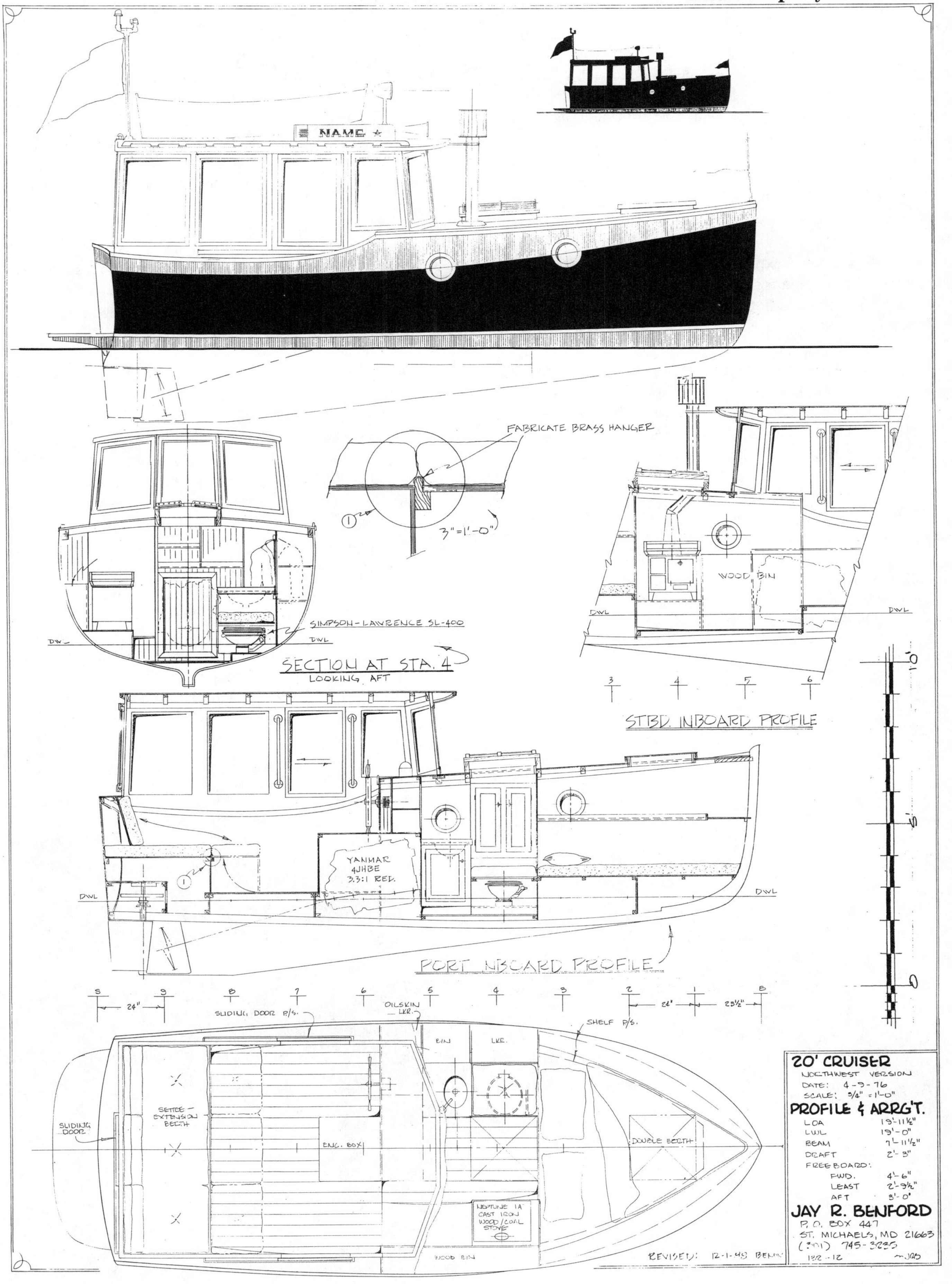

FABRICATE BRASS HANGER

$3" = 1'-0"$

SIMPSON-LAWRENCE SL-400

WOOD BIN

DWL

DWL

SECTION AT STA. 4
LOOKING AFT

3 4 5 6

STBD. INBOARD PROFILE

YANMAR
4JHBE
3.3:1 RED.

DWL

DWL

PORT INBOARD PROFILE

9 9 8 7 6 5 4 3 2 B

24"

SLIDING DOOR P/S.

OILSKIN
LKR.

24" 20½"

SHELF P/S.

BIN LKR.

SLIDING
DOOR

SETTEE-
EXTENSION
BERTH

ENG. BOX

DOUBLE BERTH

NEPTUNE 1A
CAST IRON
WOOD/COAL
STOVE

WOOD BIN

REVISED: 12-1-48 BENM

20' CRUISER
NORTHWEST VERSION
DATE: 4-9-76
SCALE: 3/4" = 1'-0"
PROFILE & ARRG'T.

LOA	19'-11½"
LWL	19'-0"
BEAM	7'-11½"
DRAFT	2'-3"
FREEBOARD:	
FWD.	4'-6"
LEAST	2'-9½"
AFT	3'-0"

JAY R. BENFORD
P.O. BOX 447
ST. MICHAELS, MD 21663
(301) 745-3235
132-12

31', 32', 35', 37', and 45' Tug Yachts

After the 38' Tugs were in production, it became obvious that there were a lot of people who would love to own one, but found the price too high. Not wanting to miss out on the possibility of making more sales, the builder commissioned us to do a couple rounds of conceptual work on both a smaller and larger version.

One of the concerns expressed to me after seeing the accommodation plan for the 31-footer was to the effect that why should anyone buy the 38-footer when they had almost the same interior on the 31...

In actuality, there is more space both inside and on deck on the 38-footer, but the essence of the 38's layout is in the 31. This layout is a variation of what is in the 32 and 35-footers, and some elements of all three arrangements are interchangeable.

The larger version was for a 45 that grew to a 48-footer. I did some design work on the 45 for building her cold-molded, and this would be quite feasible.

Although originally intended for Airex-cored 'glass construction, they could be readily built of a combination of strip-planking and cold-molding.

We later had a client who wanted a tug about this size in steel, and the 32' version was the result. Several of these have been built, and at least one was done with the house and interior layout from the 31-footer. (See photo)

The 35' Tug was done for a friend who built husky wooden vessels. He wanted to get some experience doing cold-molding while he built himself a working tug he could use for other projects. So far, though, he's not had the time to get the tug built.

However, we've had others interested in the design since then, and have also done an Airex-cored 'glass version of her. Her layout is a variation on the others in this size range, and shows another alternative on what can be done within this house.

The 37-footer was done for a fellow who wanted to use it for a little light towing, salvage and diving work. This led to the longer working deck aft. The twin engines will be able to do more work as a tug, or let her run a bit faster than a conventional displacement hull, when running light. Her hull form has the buttocks kept immersed aft, so the stern shouldn't settle too much as she's powered up to speed.

The single screw version of the 37' tug is wider, which gives her greater stability to carry the taller houses. They are very roomy and would make a nice liveaboard. The original intention was for using her to carry groups of up to 20 passengers on harbor tours, and providing separate living quarters forward for the crew. A simple rearrangement would make for a nice family room in the saloon, with room for both dining and lounging.

The completed steel hull and deck for Harland Domke's 32' tug is hauled off to the outfitting site (left). Bill Burtis's MAGGIE (above) does some charter work. Bob Bichan's KRISTIN B (below) has lots of room for carrying a group of friends.

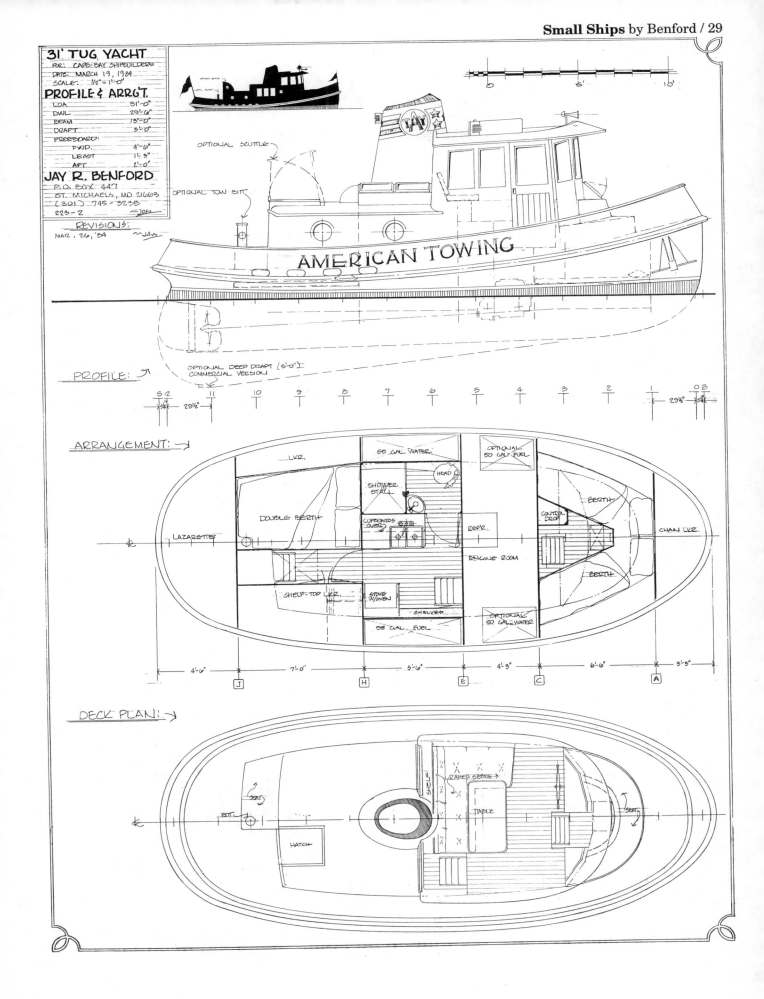

31' TUG YACHT

FOR: CAPE BAY SHIPBUILDERS
DATE: MARCH 19, 1984
SCALE: 1½"=1'-0"

PROFILE & ARRG'T.

LOA	31'-0"
DWL	29'-6"
BEAM	13'-0"
DRAFT	3'-0"
FREEBOARD:	
FWD.	4'-6"
LEAST	1'-3"
AFT	2'-0"

JAY R. BENFORD
P.O. BOX 447
ST. MICHAELS, MD 21663
(301) 745-3235
223-2

REVISIONS:
MAR. 26, '84

OPTIONAL SCUTTLE

OPTIONAL TOW BITT

AMERICAN TOWING

PROFILE:

OPTIONAL DEEP DRAFT (5'-0")
COMMERCIAL VERSION

S 12   11   10   9   8   7   6   5   4   3   2   1   0 B

ARRANGEMENT:

LKR.   55 GAL. WATER   OPTIONAL 50 GAL. FUEL
SHOWER STALL   HEAD
DOUBLE BERTH   BERTH
CUPBOARDS OVER   CONTROL DROP
LAZARETTE   REFR.   CHAIN LKR.
ENGINE ROOM   BERTH
SHELF-TOP LKR.   STOVE W/OVEN   SHELVES
55 GAL. FUEL   OPTIONAL 50 GAL. WATER

4'-6"   7'-0"   5'-6"   4'-3"   6'-6"   3'-3"
J   H   E   C   A

DECK PLAN:

RAISED SETTEE
SEAT   SHELF   SEAT
BITT   TABLE
HATCH

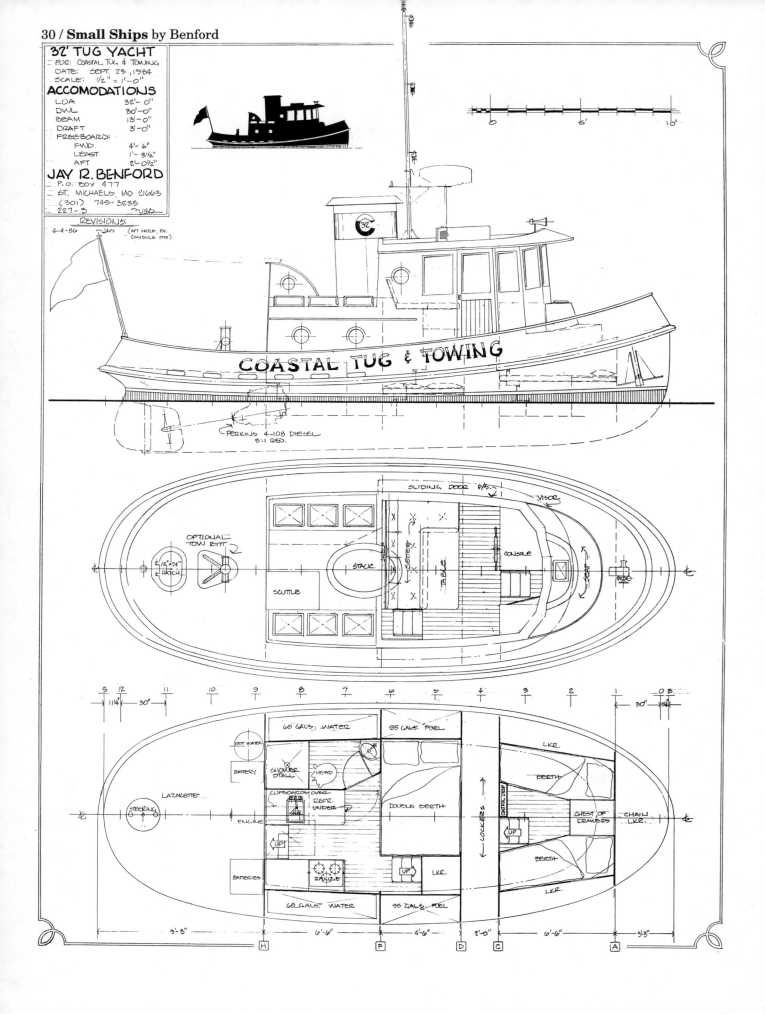

32' TUG YACHT
- FOR: COASTAL TUG & TOWING
- DATE: SEPT. 23, 1984
- SCALE: 1/2" = 1'-0"

ACCOMODATIONS

LOA	32'-0"
DWL	30'-0"
BEAM	13'-0"
DRAFT	3'-0"
FREEBOARD:	
FWD.	4'-6"
LEAST	1'-3 1/2"
AFT	2'-0 1/2"

JAY R. BENFORD
P.O. BOX 477
ST. MICHAELS, MD 21663
(301) 745-3235
227-3

REVISIONS:
4-4-86   JRB   (AFT HATCH, RH.
                   CONSOLE STBD)

COASTAL TUG & TOWING

PERKINS 4-108 DIESEL
3:1 RED.

SLIDING DOOR P/S.
VISOR
OPTIONAL TOW BITT
15"×24" HATCH
STACK
SCUTTLE
CONSOLE
SEAT
TABLE

65 GALS. WATER   95 GALS. FUEL
HOT WATER   LKR.
BATTERY   BERTH
SHOWER STALL   HEAD
LAZARETTE   CUPBOARDS   OVER REFR. UNDER   DOUBLE BERTH   CHEST OF DRAWERS   CHAIN LKR.
STEERING   LOCKERS   UP
ENGINE   UP   BERTH
                SINK
BATTERIES   RANGE   UP   LKR.
               65 GALS. WATER   95 GALS. FUEL   LKR.

9'-3"   6'-6"   4'-6"   2'-0"   6'-6"   3'-3"
H   F   D   C   A

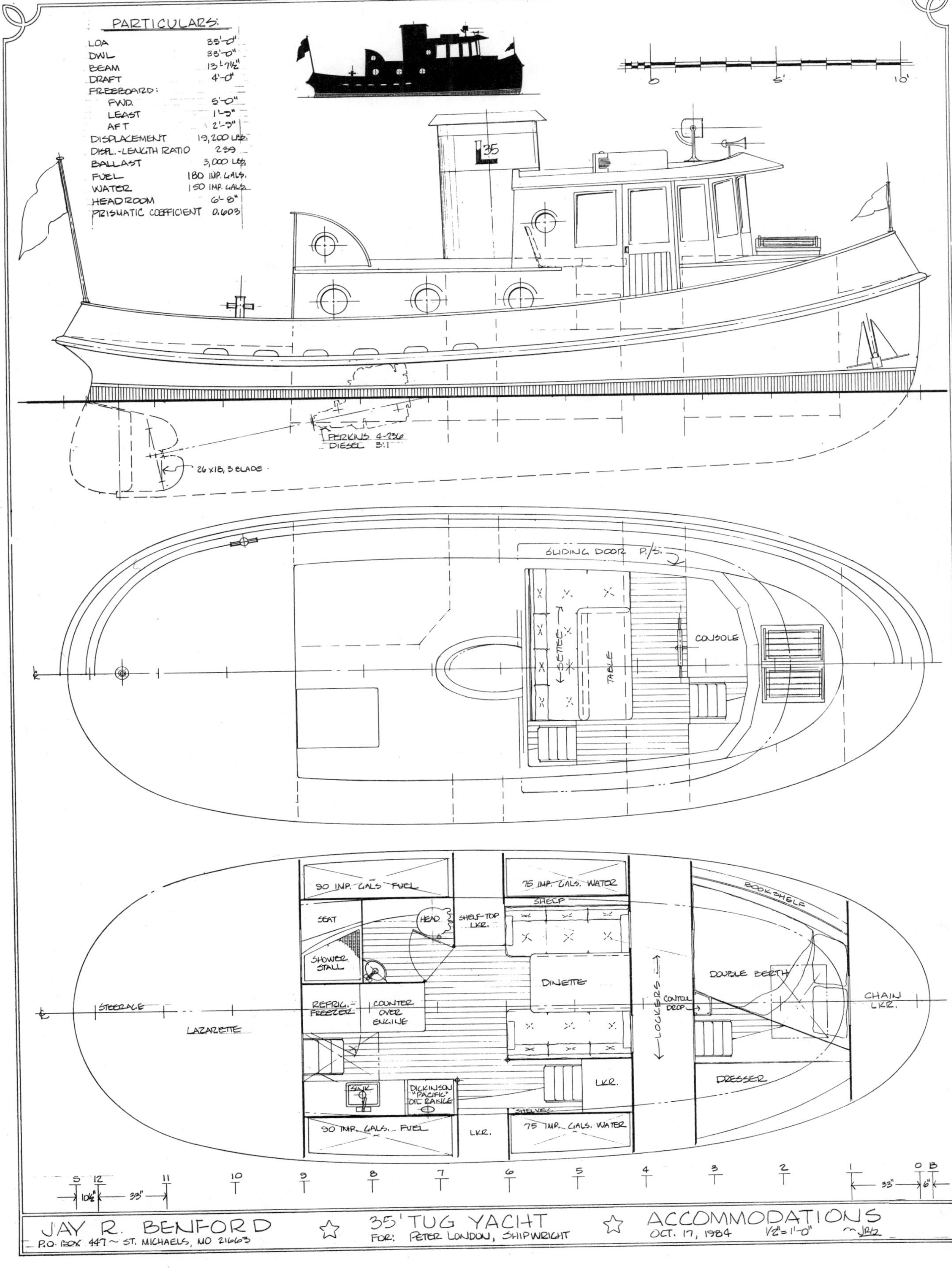

PARTICULARS:
LOA 35'-0"
DWL 33'-0"
BEAM 13'-7½"
DRAFT 4'-0"
FREEBOARD:
FWD. 5'-0"
LEAST 1'-5"
AFT 2'-9"
DISPLACEMENT 19,200 LBS.
DISPL.-LENGTH RATIO 239
BALLAST 3,000 LBS.
FUEL 180 IMP. GALS.
WATER 150 IMP. GALS.
HEADROOM 6'-8"
PRISMATIC COEFFICIENT 0.603
0 5' 10'
35
PERKINS 4-236
DIESEL 3:1
26 X 18, 3 BLADE
SLIDING DOOR P/S.
SETTEE
TABLE
CONSOLE
90 IMP. GALS. FUEL
75 IMP. GALS. WATER
SHELF
BOOKSHELF
SEAT
HEAD
SHELF-TOP LKR.
SHOWER STALL
DINETTE
DOUBLE BERTH
REFRIG. FREEZER
COUNTER OVER ENGINE
CONTROL DROP
CHAIN LKR.
STEERAGE
LAZARETTE
LOCKERS
SINK
DICKINSON "PACIFIC" OIL RANGE
LKR.
DRESSER
SHELVES
90 IMP. GALS. FUEL
LKR.
75 IMP. GALS. WATER
S 12 11 10 9 8 7 6 5 4 3 2 1 0 B
10½" 33" 33" 6"
JAY R. BENFORD
P.O. BOX 447 ~ ST. MICHAELS, MD 21663
35' TUG YACHT
FOR: PETER LONDON, SHIPWRIGHT
ACCOMMODATIONS
OCT. 17, 1984 ½"=1'-0"
JRB

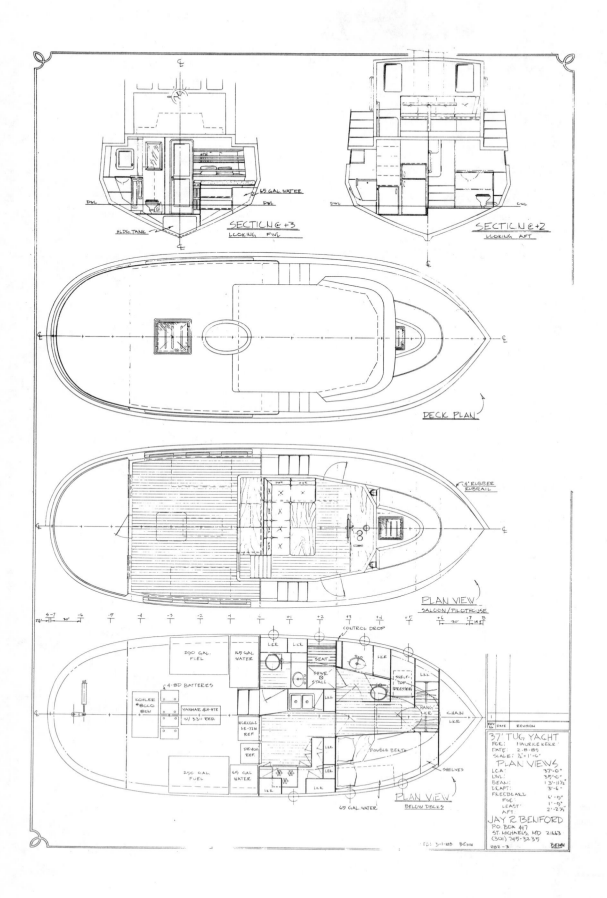

SECTION @ +3
LOOKING FWD

SECTION @ +2
LOOKING AFT

DECK PLAN

PLAN VIEW
SALOON / PILOTHOUSE

PLAN VIEW
BELOW DECKS

37' TUG YACHT
FOR: MAURICE KERR
DATE: 2-8-85
SCALE: ½"=1'-0"
PLAN VIEWS
LOA: 37'-0"
LWL: 35'-0"
BEAM: 13'-11½"
DRAFT: 3'-6"
FREEBOARD
  FWD: 6'-5"
  LEAST: 1'-5"
  AFT: 2'-2½"
JAY R BENFORD
P.O. BOX 447
ST. MICHAELS, MD 21663
(301) 745-3235

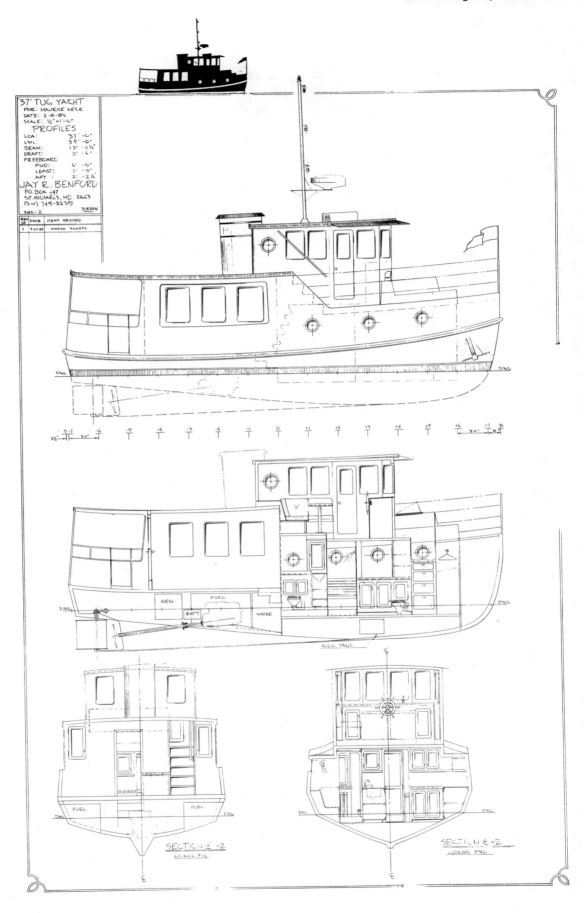

37' TUG YACHT
FOR: MAURICE KERR
DATE: 2-8-89
SCALE: 1/2"=1'-0"
PROFILES
LOA: 37'-0"
LWL: 35'-0"
BEAM: 13'-11½"
DRAFT: 3'-6"
FREEBOARD
  FWD: 6'-9"
  LEAST: 1'-9"
  AFT: 2'-2½"
JAY R. BENFORD
P.O. BOX 447
ST.MICHAELS, MD 21663
(301) 745-3235

SECTION @ -2
LOOKING FWD.

SECTION @ +2
LOOKING FWD.

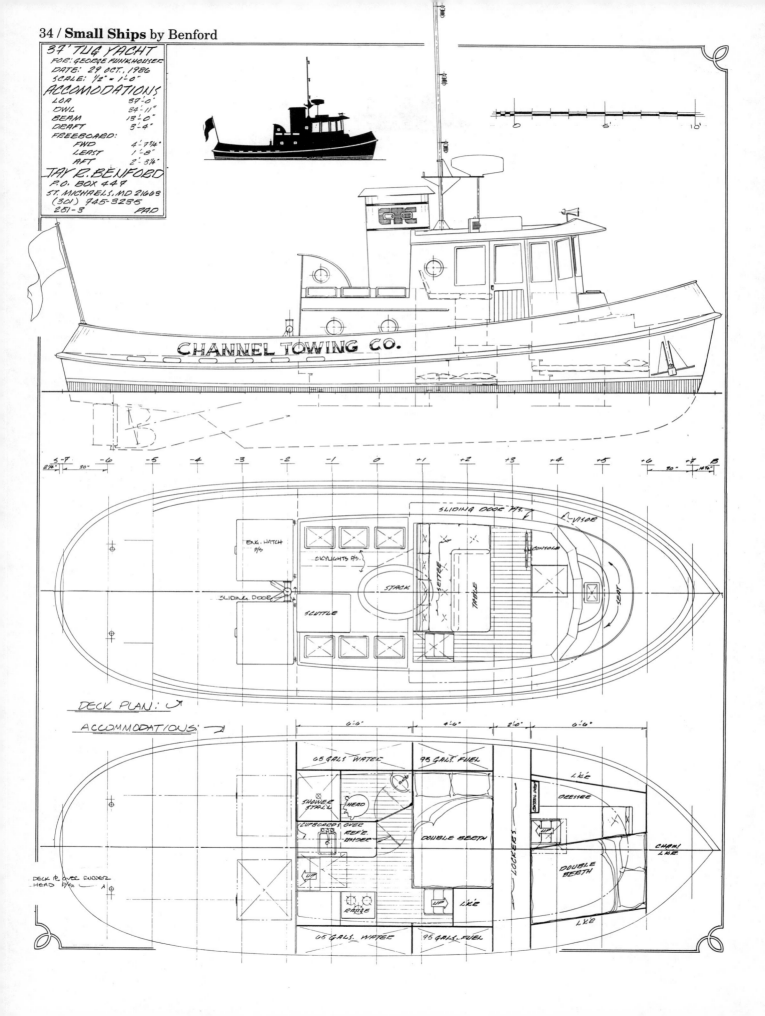

37' TUG YACHT
FOR: GEORGE FUNKHOUSER
DATE: 29 OCT., 1986
SCALE: ½" = 1'-0"

ACCOMODATIONS

LOA	37'-0"
DWL	34'-11"
BEAM	13'-0"
DRAFT	3'-4"
FREEBOARD:	
FWD	4'-7¾"
LEAST	1'-8"
AFT	2'-3¼"

JAY R. BENFORD
P.O. BOX 447
ST. MICHAELS, MD 21663
(301) 745-3235
251-3   PAD

CHANNEL TOWING CO.

DECK PLAN:

ACCOMMODATIONS:

SLIDING DOOR P/S.
ENG. HATCH P/S
SKYLIGHTS P/S.
SLIDING DOOR
SCUTTLE
STACK
SETTEE
TABLE
CONSOLE
VISOR
SEAT

65 GALS WATER
95 GALS. FUEL
L'K'E
SHOWER STALL
HEAD
DRESSER
CUPBOARDS OVER REFR. UNDER
DOUBLE BERTH
CHAIN L'K'E
RANGE
L'K'E
LOCKERS
DOUBLE BERTH
L'K'E
DECK R OVER RUDDER HEAD P/S
65 GALS. WATER
95 GALS. FUEL
L'K'E

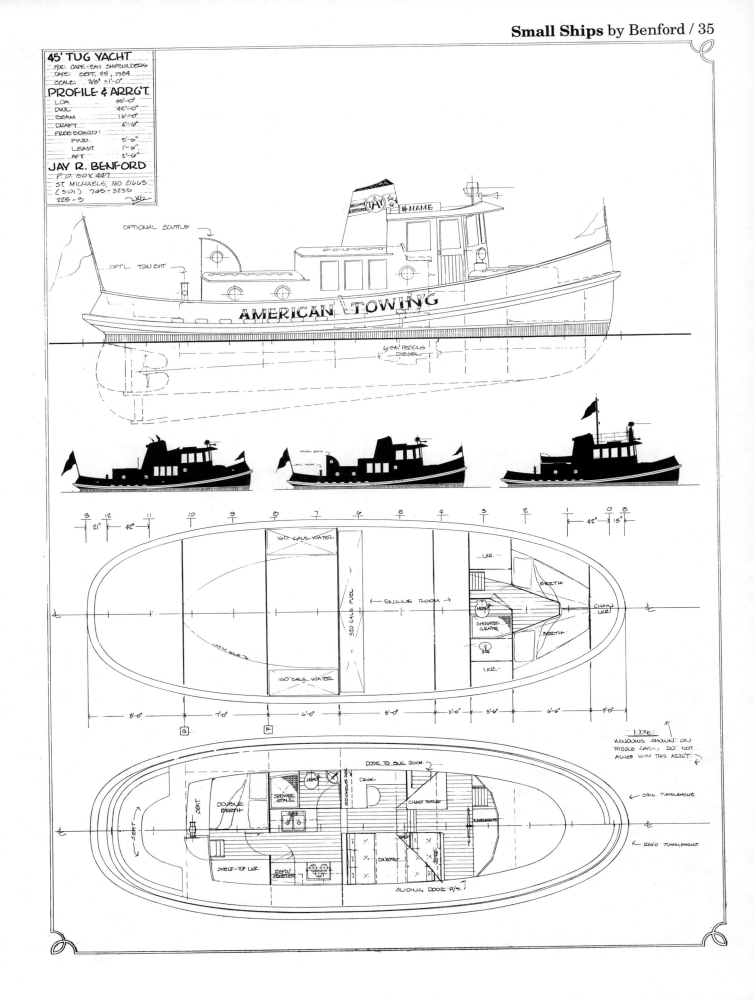

45' TUG YACHT
FOR: CAPE-BAY SHIPBUILDERS
DATE: SEPT. 25, 1984
SCALE: 3/8" = 1'-0"

PROFILE & ARRG'T.

LOA	45'-0"
DWL	42'-0"
BEAM	16'-0"
DRAFT	4'-6"
FREEBOARD:	
FWD.	5'-6"
LEAST	1'-6"
AFT	2'-6"

JAY R. BENFORD
P.O. BOX 447
ST. MICHAELS, MD 21663
(301) 745-3235
228-3

American Tug-Yacht 38

My late friend Ron Brown and I evolved this design over a period of time. The more we talked about it, the more ideas we came up with for evolutionary improvements.

Ron liked the way this boat exuded the "true tug" look of the working tugs we'd seen in the major seaports. He felt that too many of the boats being offered as tug yachts were simply trawler yachts with a stack tacked on for looks. I agreed, and drew on the tugs I'd worked on at Foss during the '60's to get the right hull form, sheer, and house proportions.

By paying particular attention to the spatial relations of the interior elements we wanted, I was able to come up with several workable layouts, depending on how the client wanted to use the boat. We were able to keep all these within the deckhouse that had the right "look." The twin skylights either side of the stack not only gave great light and ventilation to the galley, but provided extra headroom so we would keep the shafts of the twin screw version under the cabin sole.

The raised settee in the pilothouse puts the passengers at a height where they can see all around. It also creates a space under it where we can have a full headroom shower stall and head.

The company Ron Brown founded built four of these tugs before his death, and I've been pleased with how the design worked out in real life. The molds have since changed hands, and these fiberglass tugs can still be built to order.

We designed a 40' barge with a 12' landing ramp and articulated push linkage for use with the 38' twin screw TUG. They work as an island support team, hauling fuel oil and a myriad of other supplies.

LOAFER is a cruising version of the 38' Tug. (These
photos were taken on trials before completion, accounting
for the missing doors.) Her wonderfully springy sheer is
well evident, and she looks every bit the descendant of the
classic working tugs. Ron and I were delighted with the
results of our work in making the "look" of these boats just
right. Photos by Monica Brown.

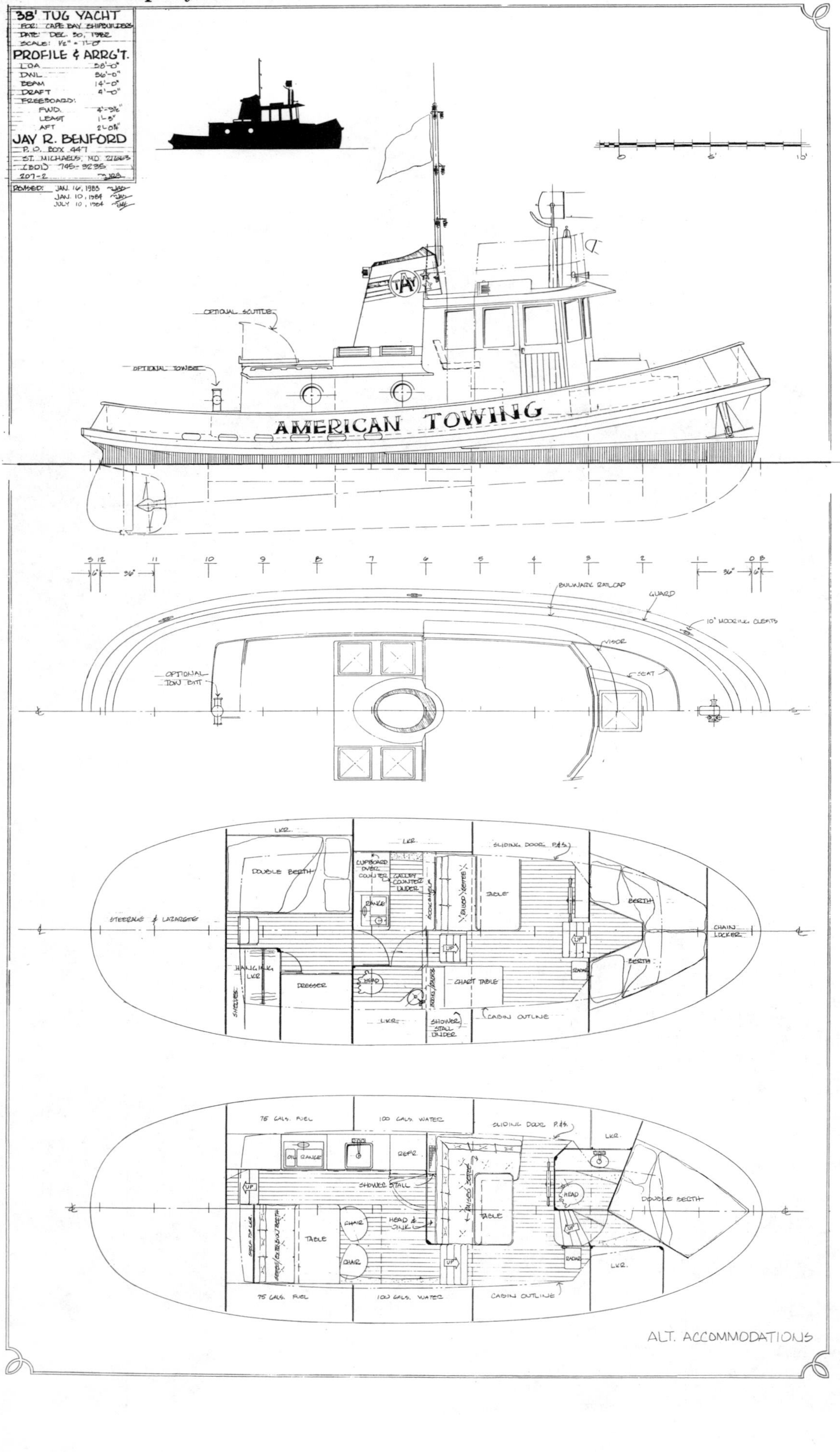

38' TUG YACHT
FOR: CAPE BAY SHIPBUILDERS
DATE: DEC. 30, 1982
SCALE: ½" = 1'-0"
PROFILE & ARRG'T.
LOA 38'-0"
DWL 36'-0"
BEAM 14'-0"
DRAFT 4'-0"
FREEBOARD:
FWD. 4'-9½"
LEAST 1'-3"
AFT 2'-0¼"
JAY R. BENFORD
P.O. BOX 447
ST. MICHAELS, MD 21663
(301) 745-3235
207-2
REVISED: JAN. 16, 1983
JAN. 10, 1984
JULY 10, 1984
OPTIONAL SCUTTLE
OPTIONAL TOWBITT
AMERICAN TOWING
BULWARK RAILCAP
GUARD
10" MOORING CLEATS
VISOR
SEAT
OPTIONAL TOW BITT
LKR
DOUBLE BERTH
CUPBOARD OVER COUNTER
GALLEY COUNTER UNDER
RANGE
TABLE
SLIDING DOOR P&S
BERTH
STEERAGE & LAZARETTE
CHAIN LOCKER
HANGING LKR
DRESSER
HEAD
CHART TABLE
SHELVES
SHOWER STALL UNDER
CABIN OUTLINE
UP
75 GALS. FUEL
100 GALS. WATER
OIL RANGE
REFR.
SHOWER STALL
HEAD & SINK
CHAIR
RADAR
ALT. ACCOMMODATIONS

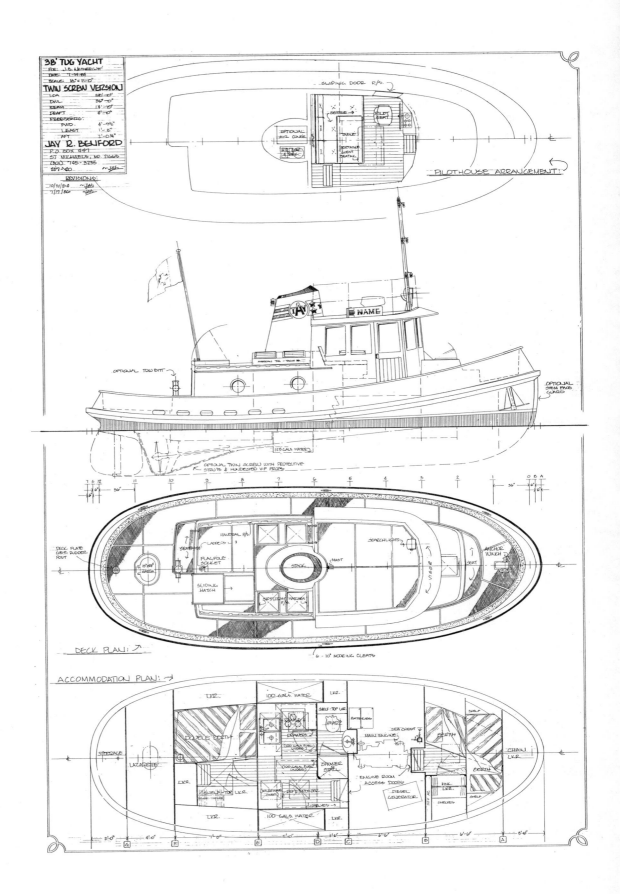

38' TUG YACHT
FOR: J.B. NETHERCUTT
DATE: 7-14-89
SCALE: 1/2" = 1'-0"
TWIN SCREW VERSION
LOA   38'-0"
DWL   36'-0"
BEAM   13'-0"
DRAFT   4'-0"
FREEBOARD:
   FWD.   4'-0½"
   LEAST   1'-8"
   AFT   2'-0¼"
JAY R. BENFORD
P.O. BOX 447
ST. MICHAELS, MD. 21663
(301) 745-3235
207-80

REVISIONS:
10/21/84
7/17/00

PILOTHOUSE ARRANGEMENT:

OPTIONAL TOW BITT

OPTIONAL STEM FACE GUARD

125 GALS WATER

OPTIONAL TWIN SCREW WITH PROTECTIVE STRUTS & HUNDESTED V-P PROPS

DECK PLAN:

ACCOMMODATION PLAN:

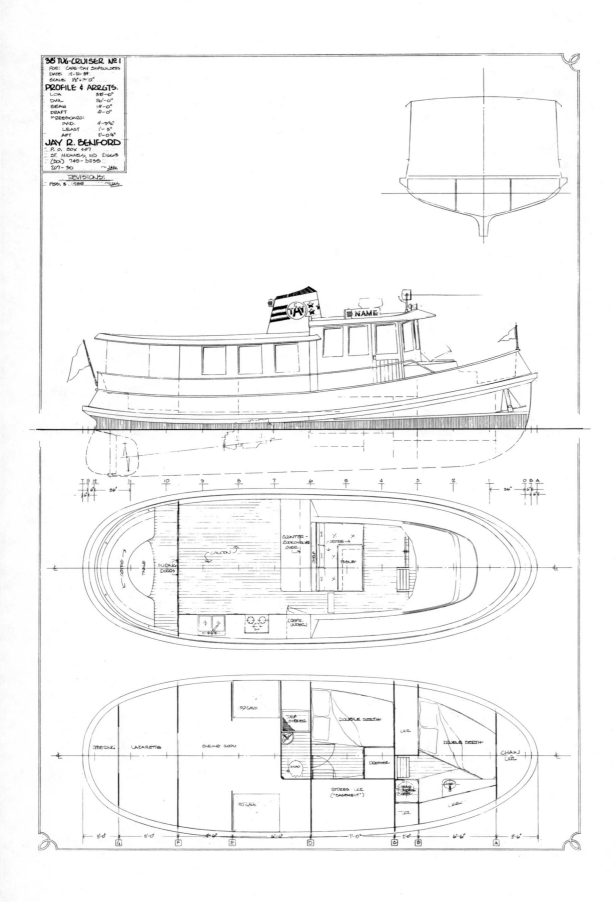

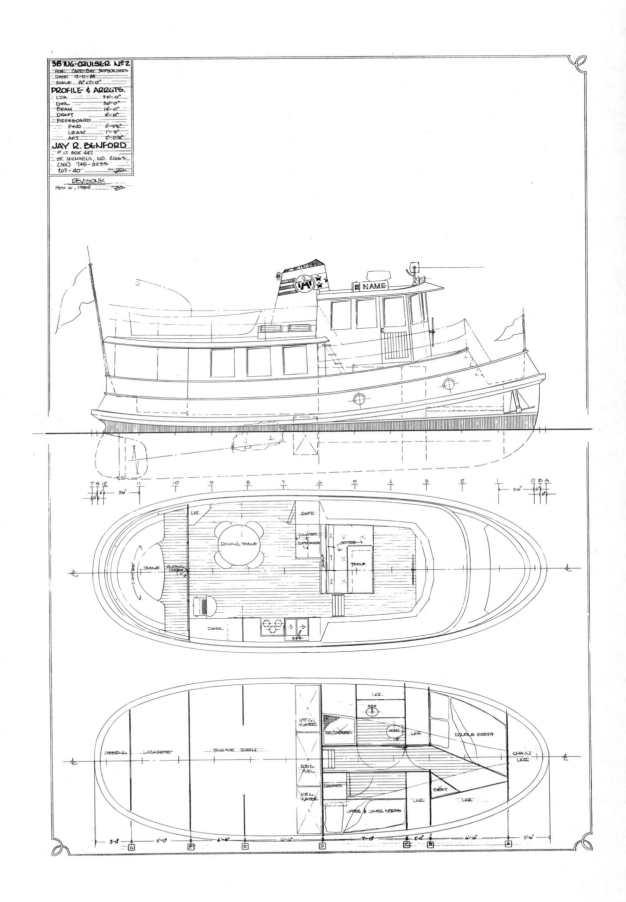

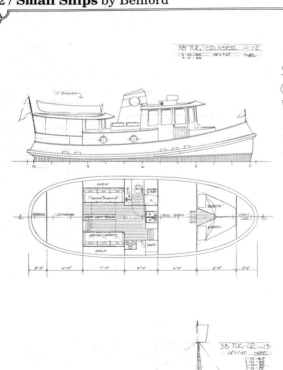

SOME VARIATIONS
ON THE 38' TUG
DESIGN —
HOW WOULD
YOU LIKE
YOURS DONE?

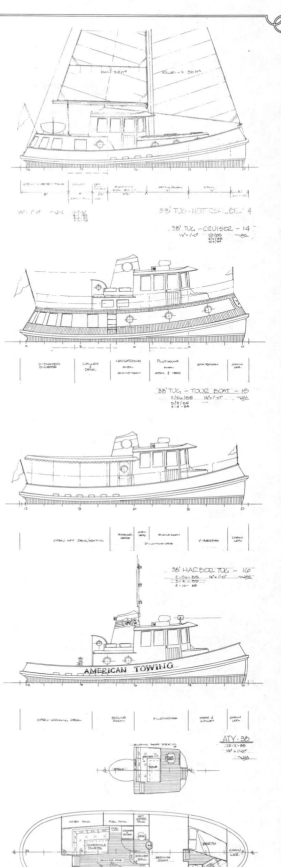

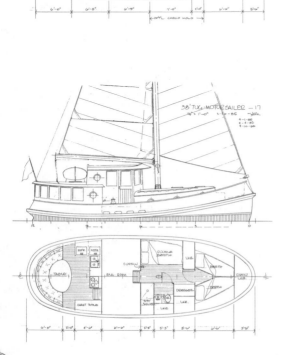

48' Tug Yacht ELIJAH CURTIS

Designed as a liveaboard on which a couple can follow the seasons up and down the East Coast, this 48-footer is a husky small ship. She has an open walkaround at main-deck level, making line handling and boarding easy. The housetop of the saloon overhangs the side and after decks, for extra shelter from sun and rain. The pilothouse is raised a few steps, and has a big ship style bridge around it.

The saloon is roomy and well lit, with windows on three sides. it contains the lounging area, the dining area, and the galley. Just a few steps down leads to the two staterooms and two heads. The forward stateroom is the master, with a private entry head. The tub and shower stall is shared between the two heads, making for one quite roomy space instead of two small stalls.

A few steps up from the saloon is the office or navigation area and the pilothouse. The oilskin locker also will serve well as a coat closet in day-to-day living aboard.

The water tanks, which will be drawn down and refilled most often, are located admidships where they will have practically no effect on fore and aft trim. We've given her fuel tanks forward, in the double bottom under the cabin sole, and aft in the corners of the engine room. By judiciously watching how these are drawn down, good fore and aft and transverse trim can be maintained, even with varying loads as the boat cruises and other things are consumed or added to her cargo.

The scantling section shown below is typical of how our freighters are done also, and will give some idea of the heft of a steel boat of this size.

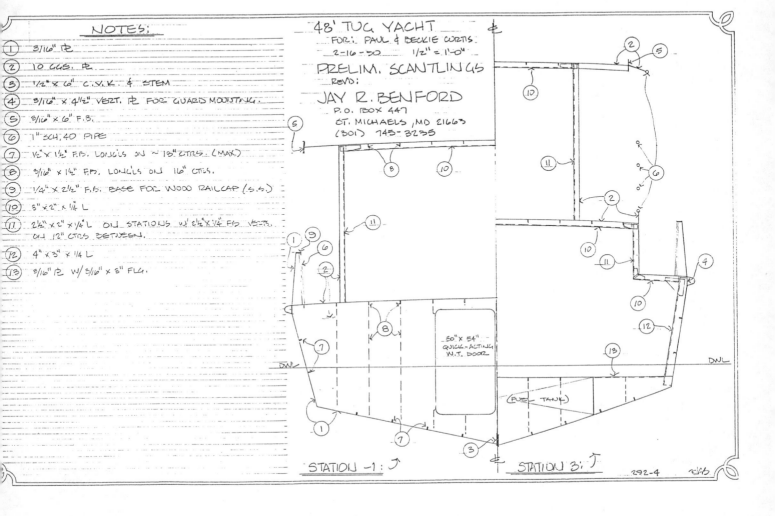

48' TUG YACHT
10/2/89   1/4" = 1'-0"
FOR: PAUL & BECKIE CURTIS
OUTBOARD PROFILE
REVISED: 11-5-89/11-26-89/2-14-90
JAY R. BENFORD
P.O. BOX 447
ST. MICHAELS, MD 21663
(301) 745-3235

11' DINGHY

ELIJAH CURTIS

ST. MICHAELS, MD

750 GALS. FUEL

S -7 -6 -5 -4 -3 -2 -1 0 1 2 3 4 5 6 7 8 B
18" 36"   36" 18"

ACCOMMODATIONS
REVISED: 11-26-89/2-14-90

SEA CHEST

OIL SKINS

UP

DOWN

DESK

SEA CHEST / SETTEE

CHART TABLE

JAY R. BENFORD
P.O. BOX 447
ST. MICHAELS, MD 21663
(301) 745-3235

S -7 -6 -5 -4 -3 -2 -1 0 1 2 3 4 5 6 7 8 B
18" 36"   36" 18"

125 G. FUEL

500 GALS. WATER

DRYER   WASHER

ENGINE ROOM

140HP YANMAR DIESEL
W/2.57:1 & 12.5 KW.
KOHLER GEN. SET

DOWN

UP

WORKBENCH

125 G. FUEL

500 GALS. WATER

LKR.

DOUBLE BERTH

DR.

HANGING LKR.

HANGING LOCKER

DRESSER

WC

TUB/SHOWER

WC

DOUBLE BERTH

CHAIN LKR.

DRESSER

LKR.

292-3

Part 3 — Freighters

The FLORIDA BAY was the first of the line of Florida Bay Coaster built, and we had a great time designing and using her. She is still my favorite of the ones we've built so far, sentimentally and esthetically. Like all of them, she exudes a solid, big ship feel, giving you the feeling you're on a much larger vessel. You step aboard, and immediately want to cast off and go cruising. It's as if she's saying to you, "Of course I can take you exploring in the places you've always wanted to see."

The design commission for the FLORIDA BAY came about from Reuben Trane seeing my 45' Friday Harbor Ferry in his search for a new liveaboard design. He liked all the room in it, but wanted to rearrange some of the spaces. And, he wanted to carry a Jeep. We went through several rounds of sketching preliminaries, and ended up with the 60-footer shown on page 77. This design was sent out for bids.

After reviewing the bids, we decided to create a smaller version, to keep the price in a more affordable range. The 50' FLORDIA BAY resulted from this, and had all the main features of the 60, with a large part of the length saved achieved by stacking the skiff over the Jeep instead of having them side by side.

I've had the pleasure of being aboard and cruising the FLORIDA BAY several times, and it's always been a delight. She has an honest and forthright appearance. Her performance lives up to it, taking you surely and safely on your way.

Small Freighters

The 35, 40, and 45-footers shown on the next several pages are some of the ideas we've been developing for a small freighter yacht. Some are shown in the rough sketch format in which we start them, and some in more polished form.

All of them represent possible solutions to getting the most livable boat for their size. My personal favorite is the 35' Packet, which I see as the logical evolution from our Friday Harbor Ferry series designed some time ago.

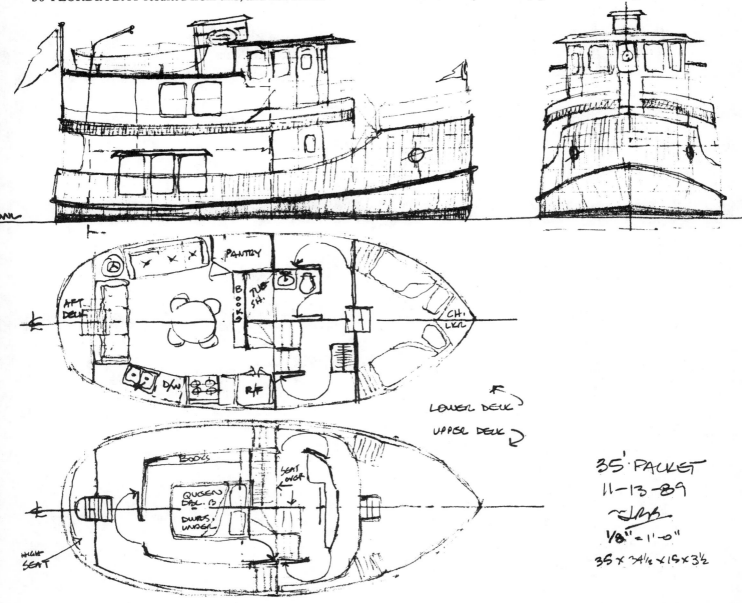

LOWER DECK

UPPER DECK

35' PACKET
11-13-89
JB
1/8" = 1'-0"
35 x 34½ x 15 x 3½

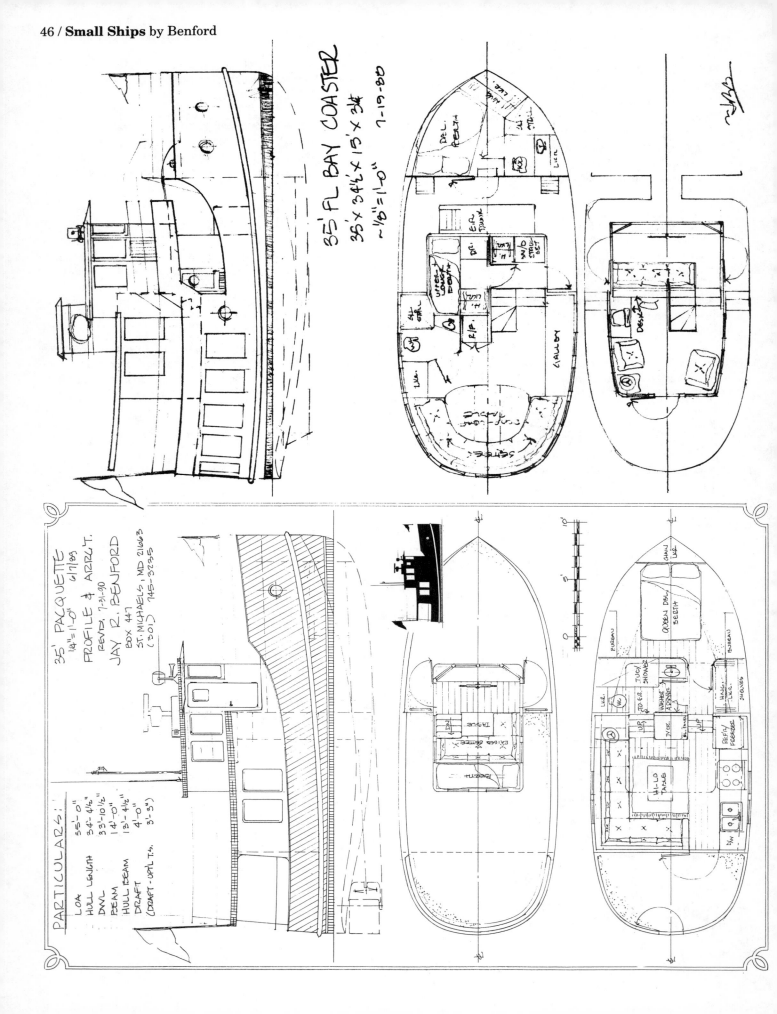

35' FL BAY COASTER
35' × 34' × 15' × 34'
~1/8" = 1'-0"
7-19-88

35' PACQUETTE
1/4" = 1'-0"
PROFILE & ARR'GT.
REVD. 7-31-90
JAY R. BENFORD
BOX 447
ST. MICHAELS, MD 21663
(301) 745-3235

PARTICULARS:
LOA   35'-0"
HULL LENGTH 34'-4 1/2"
DWL   33'-10 1/2"
BEAM   14'-0"
HULL BEAM   13'-4 1/2"
DRAFT   4'-0"
(DRAFT - UPL. T.S. 3'-5")

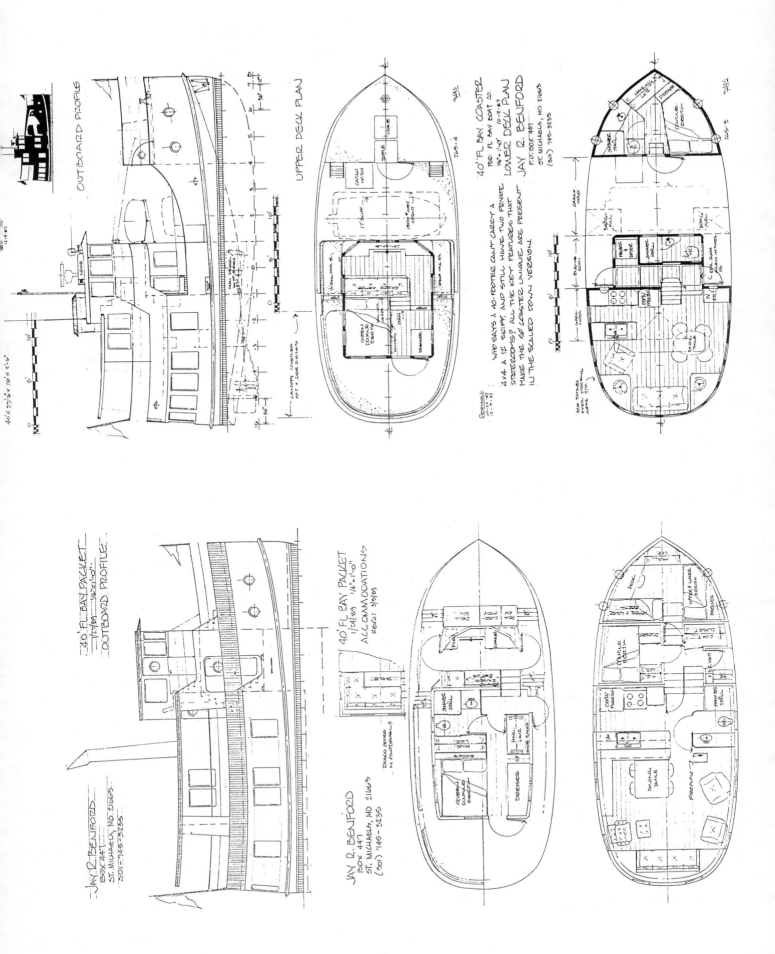

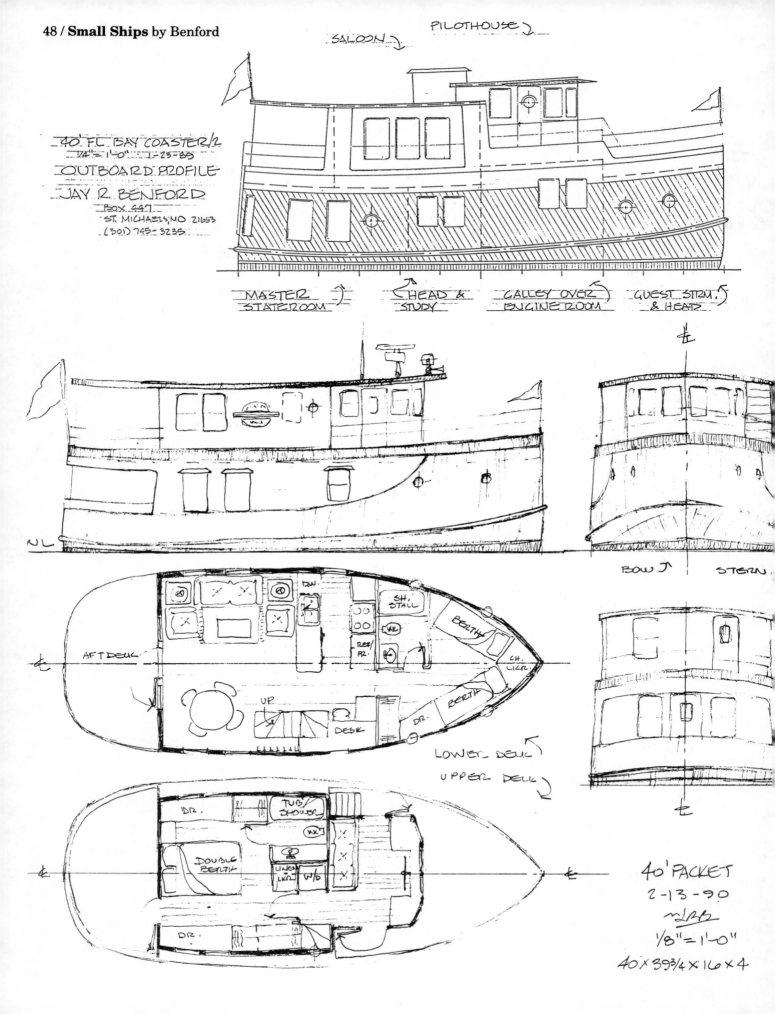

SALOON

PILOTHOUSE

40' FL BAY COASTER/2
1/4" = 1'-0"   1-23-89
OUTBOARD PROFILE
JAY R. BENFORD
BOX 447
ST. MICHAELS, MD 21663
(301) 745-3235

MASTER STATEROOM

HEAD & STUDY

GALLEY OVER ENGINE ROOM

GUEST STRM & HEADS

BOW

STERN

AFT DECK

SH. STALL
BERTH
DW
REF/FZ.
CH. LKR.
UP
DESK
DR.
BERTH

LOWER DECK
UPPER DECK

DR.
TUB/SHOWER
WC
DOUBLE BERTH
LINEN LKR.
W/D
DR.

40' PACKET
2-13-90
JRB
1/8" = 1'-0"
40 x 39 3/4 x 16 x 4

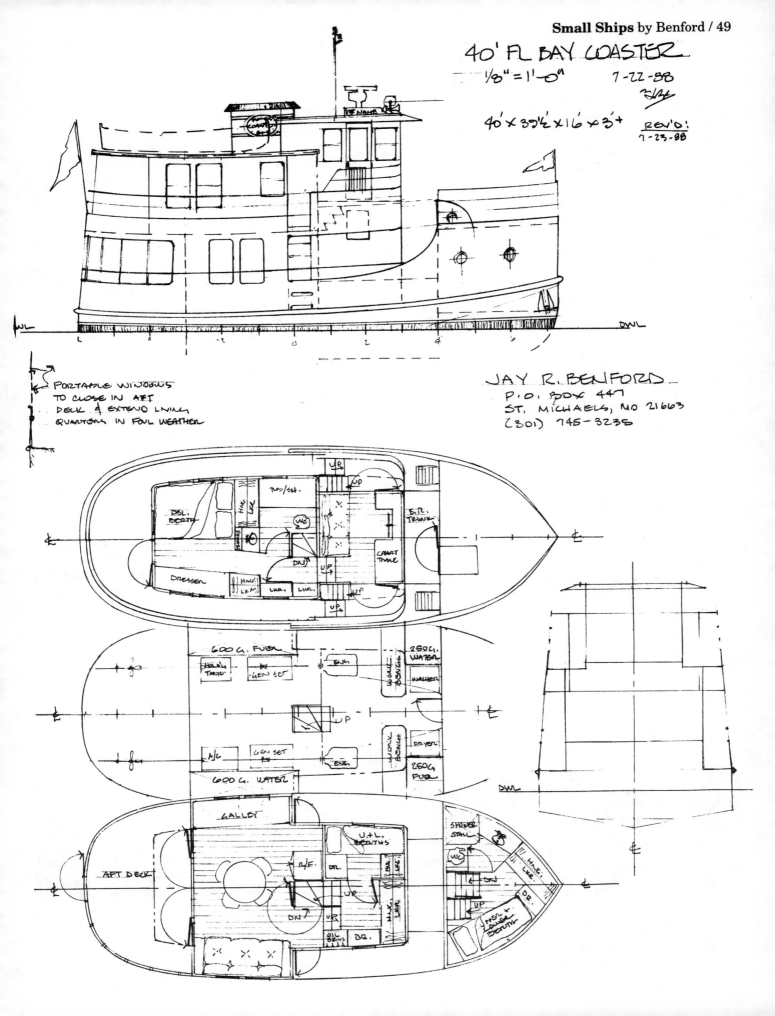

40' FL BAY COASTER

1/8" = 1'-0"   7-22-88

40' × 39'½ × 16' × 3'+   REV'D:
7-23-88

PORTABLE WINDOWS
TO CLOSE IN AFT
DECK & EXTEND LIVING
QUARTERS IN FOUL WEATHER

JAY R. BENFORD
P.O. BOX 447
ST. MICHAELS, MD 21663
(301) 745-3235

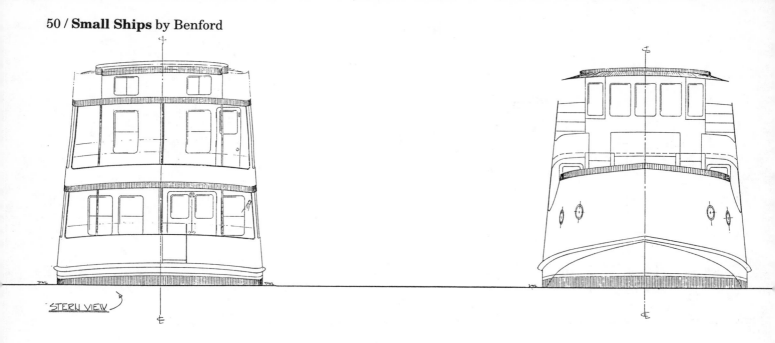

STERN VIEW

45' Florida Bay Coaster SAILS

SAILS was the first of three 45-footers of similar design recently delivered. Bow and stern view drawings of her are shown on this page, along with the photos.

SAILS was the first of the Florida Bay Coasters built without a crane and vehicle on deck. Closing up the well deck gave extra room inside, making her at least as roomy as the 50' FLORIDA BAY.

The drawings on the next page show a slightly revised version of SAILS. The second 45 was built with the Florida Room master stateroom variation. The third had the master laid out like the Bay Window version, with the head and stateroom similar to the 65' KEY LARGO.

Following on from there are a variety of other versions in this size showing how the variations possible are limited only by the imagination. Many of these are ideas I spent time on while thinking about how I would like to have one laid out for myself and my family. The 45' East Coaster PELICAN is my favorite of the variations, though the 45' Tramp is a close second.

The 48' and 52' Fantail Houseyachts are extensions of the 45-footer, with my favorite stern shape. The 52-footer also has the bow extended, making for a finer entry and easier powering. Many of the ideas shown on them can also be incorporated on the 45-footers.

SAILS on completion of her delivery trip to St. Petersburg, laid alongside the 65' KEY LARGO for a visit and then shifted to her end moorage slip, where she has an excellent

view of Tampa Bay. Note how she has almost the same height as the 65-footer, giving her generous headroom, yet maintaining good stability.

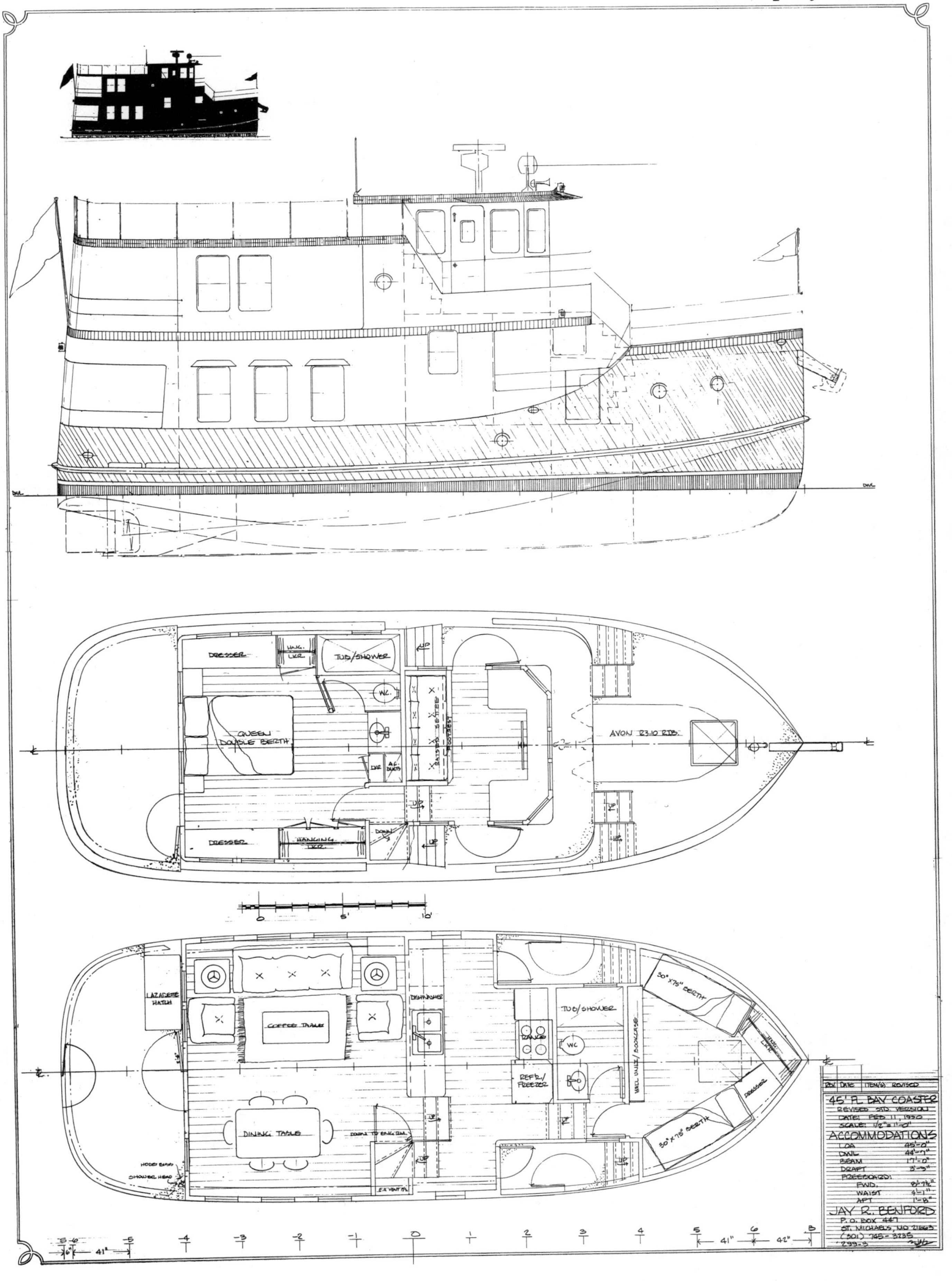

Labels on accommodation plans:

DRESSER · HNG. LKR · TUB/SHOWER · W.C. · QUEEN DOUBLE BERTH · RAISED SETTEE · DR · AC DUCTS · DRESSER · HANGING LKR · DOWN · UP · AVON R3.10 RIB

LAZARETTE HATCH · COFFEE TABLE · DISHWASHER · TUB/SHOWER · 30" × 78" BERTH · RANGE · W.C. · REFR/FREEZER · VERL DUCT/BOOKCASE · DINING TABLE · DOWN TO ENGINE RM · 30" × 78" BERTH · MODEL BENCH · SHOWER HEAD · SEA VENT RM

45' FT. BAY COASTER
REVISED STD. VERSION
DATE FEB 11 1990
SCALE: 1/2" = 1'-0"

ACCOMMODATIONS

LOA	45'-0"
DWL	44'-1"
BEAM	17'-0"
DRAFT	5'-3"
FREEBOARD:	
FWD.	8'-7½"
WAIST	4'-1"
AFT	7'-8"

JAY R. BENFORD
P. O. BOX 447
ST. MICHAELS, MD 21663
(301) 745-3235
299-5

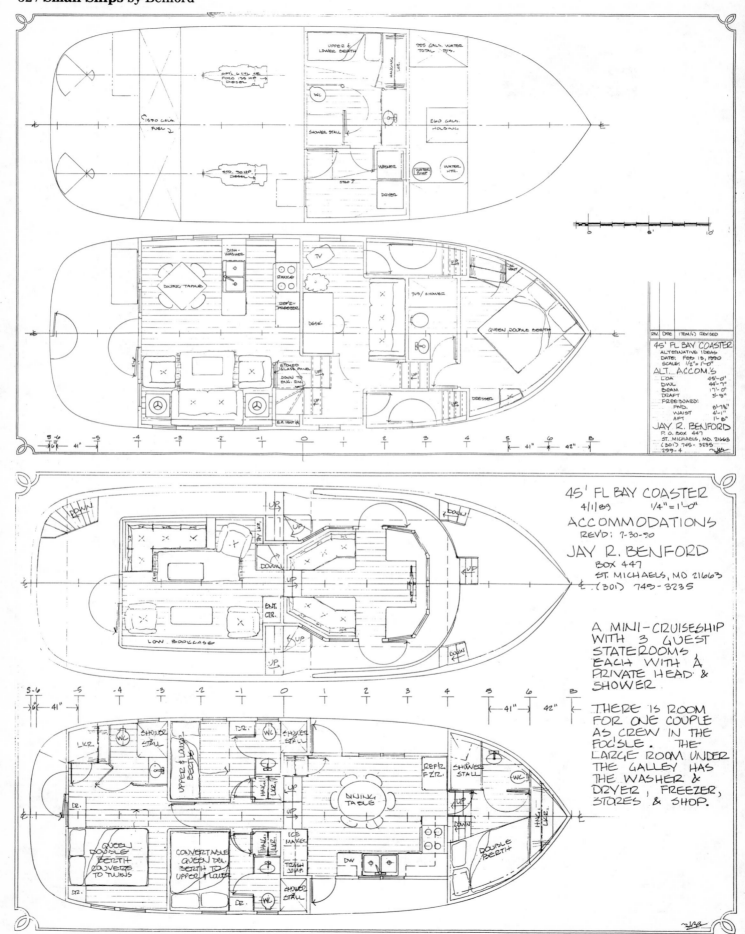

45' FL BAY COASTER
ALTERNATIVE IDEAS
DATE: FEB 13, 1990
SCALE: 1/2" = 1'-0"
ALT. ACCOM'S
LOA   45'-0"
DWL   44'-7"
BEAM   17'-0"
DRAFT   3'-9"
FREEBOARD:
   FWD.   8'-7½"
   WAIST   4'-1"
   AFT   1'-8"
JAY R. BENFORD
P.O. BOX 447
ST. MICHAELS, MD 21663
(301) 745-3235
299-4

45' FL BAY COASTER
4/1/89   1/4" = 1'-0"
ACCOMMODATIONS
REV'D: 7-30-90
JAY R. BENFORD
BOX 447
ST. MICHAELS, MD 21663
(301) 745-3235

A MINI-CRUISESHIP WITH 3 GUEST STATEROOMS EACH WITH A PRIVATE HEAD & SHOWER.

THERE IS ROOM FOR ONE COUPLE AS CREW IN THE FOC'SLE. THE LARGE ROOM UNDER THE GALLEY HAS THE WASHER & DRYER, FREEZER, STORES & SHOP.

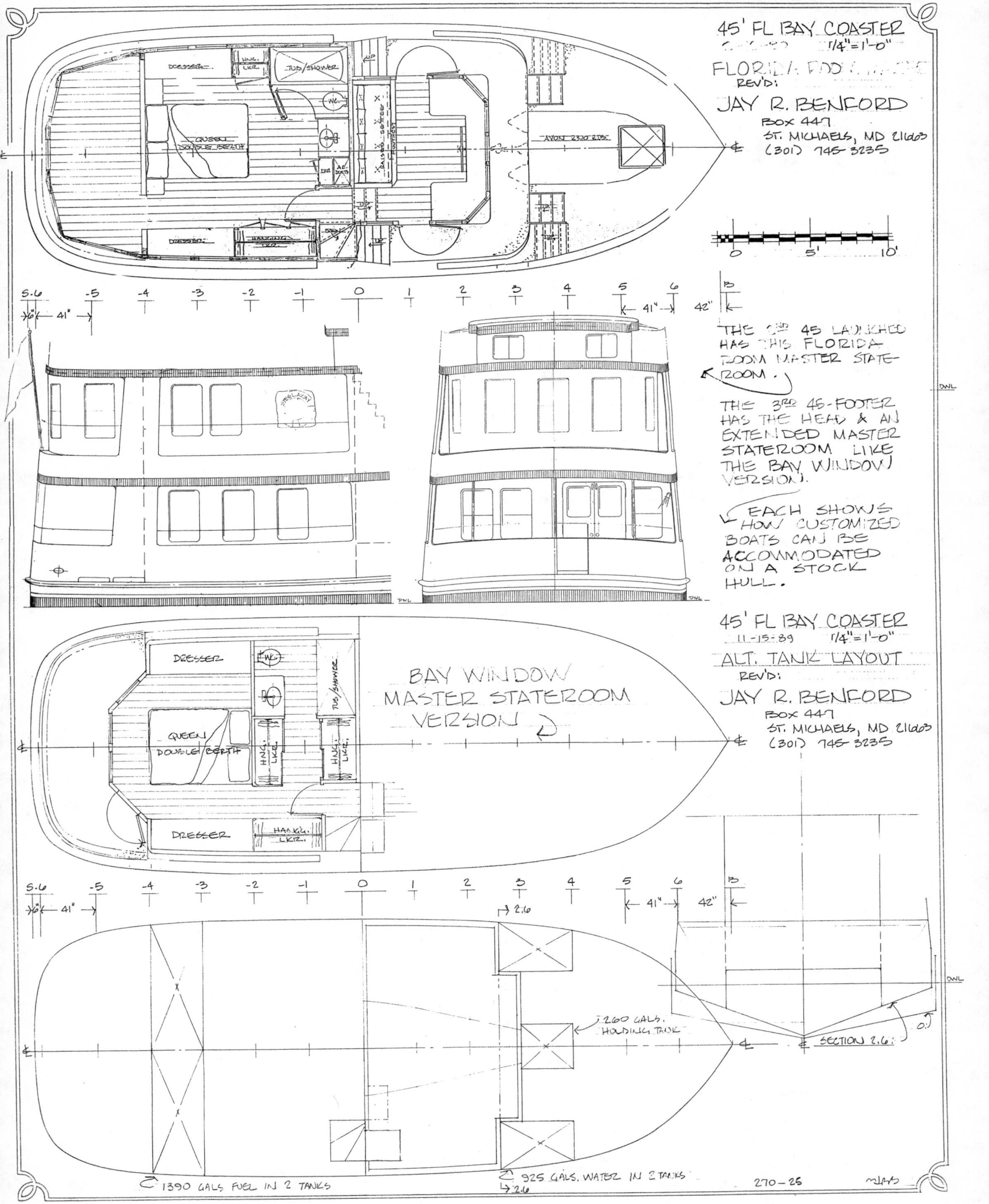

45' FL BAY COASTER

1/4"=1'-0"

FLORIDA ROOM VERSION

REV'D:

JAY R. BENFORD
BOX 447
ST. MICHAELS, MD 21663
(301) 745-3235

DRESSER

HNG.
LKR.

TUB/SHOWER

UP

W.C.

SALON & SETTEE

AVON 2310 273S

QUEEN
DOUBLE BERTH

DRESSER

HANGING
LKR.

THE 2ND 45 LAUNCHED
HAS THIS FLORIDA
ROOM MASTER STATE-
ROOM.

THE 3RD 45-FOOTER
HAS THE HEAD & AN
EXTENDED MASTER
STATEROOM LIKE
THE BAY WINDOW
VERSION.

EACH SHOWS
HOW CUSTOMIZED
BOATS CAN BE
ACCOMMODATED
ON A STOCK
HULL.

45' FL BAY COASTER

11-15-89   1/4"=1'-0"

ALT. TANK LAYOUT

REV'D:

JAY R. BENFORD
BOX 447
ST. MICHAELS, MD 21663
(301) 745-3235

DRESSER

W.C.

TUB/SHOWER

BAY WINDOW
MASTER STATEROOM
VERSION

QUEEN
DOUBLE BERTH

HNG.
LKR.

HNG.
LKR.

DRESSER

HANG.
LKR.

260 GALS.
HOLDING TANK

SECTION 2.6:

1390 GALS FUEL IN 2 TANKS

925 GALS. WATER IN 2 TANKS

270-25   JAYS

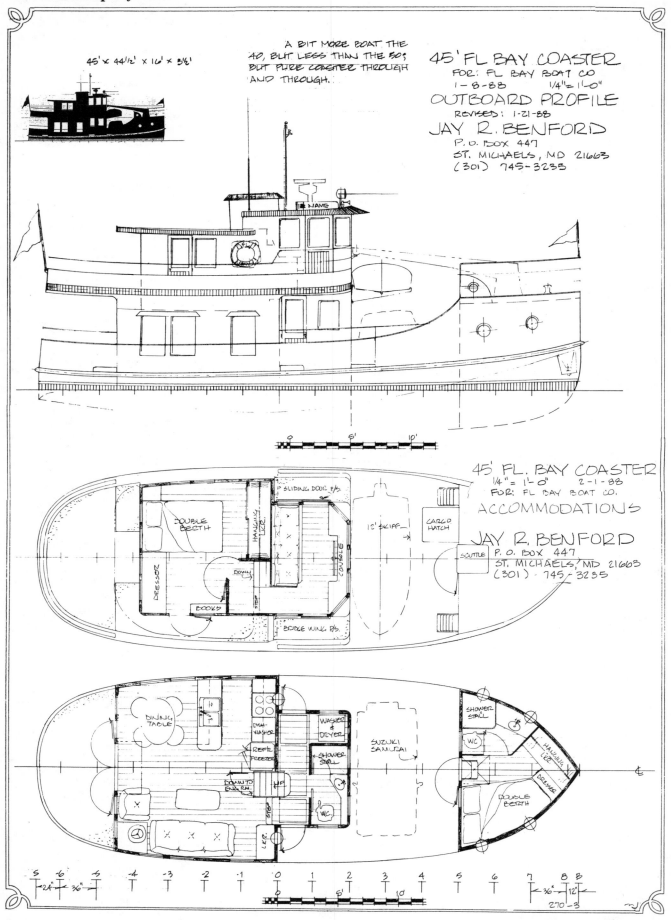

45' × 44½' × 16' × 3½'

A BIT MORE BOAT THE 40, BUT LESS THAN THE 50; BUT PURE COASTER THROUGH AND THROUGH.

45' FL BAY COASTER
FOR: FL BAY BOAT CO
1-8-88   ¼"=1'-0"
OUTBOARD PROFILE
REVISED: 1-21-88
JAY R. BENFORD
P. O. BOX 447
ST. MICHAELS, MD 21663
(301) 745-3235

NAME

45' FL. BAY COASTER
¼"=1'-0"   2-1-88
FOR: FL BAY BOAT CO.
ACCOMMODATIONS

JAY R. BENFORD
P. O. BOX 447
ST. MICHAELS, MD 21663
(301) - 745-3235

SLIDING DOOR P/S
DOUBLE BERTH
HANGING LKR.
CONSOLE
12' SKIFF
CARGO HATCH
SCUTTLE
DRESSER
DOWN
STEP
BOOKS
BRIDGE WING P/S

DINING TABLE
DISH-WASHER
REFR. FREEZER
WASHER & DRYER
SHOWER STALL
SUZUKI SAMURAI
SHOWER STALL
WC
HANGING LKR.
DOWN TO ENG. RM.
STEP
LKR.
WC
DRESSER
DOUBLE BERTH

270-3

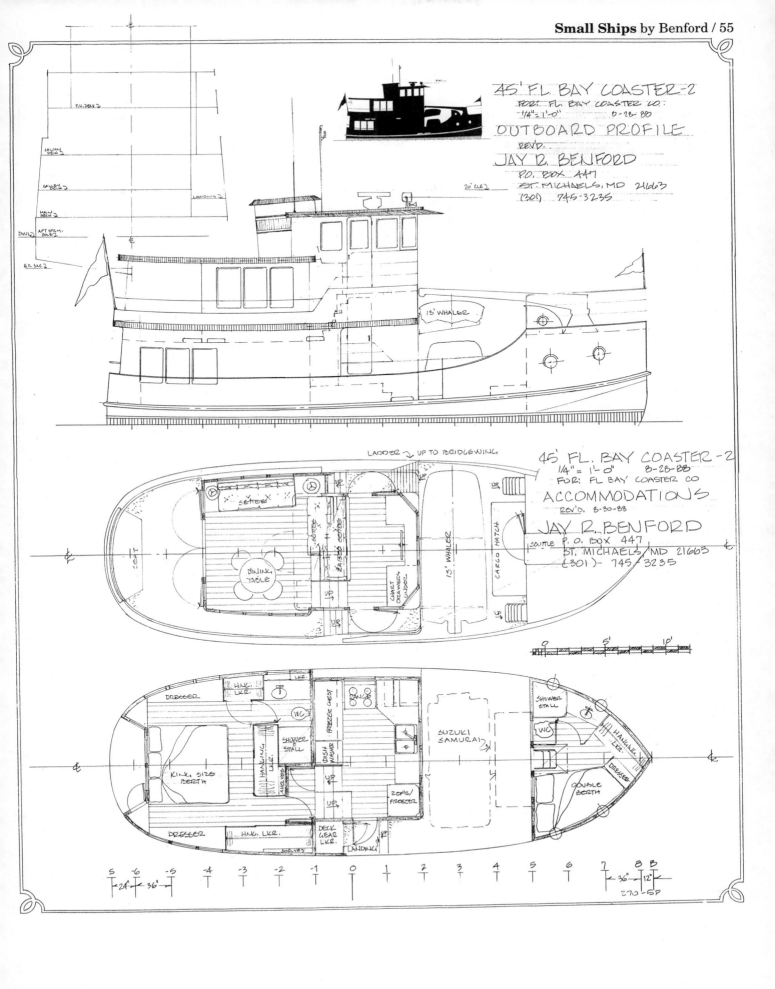

45' FL. BAY COASTER-2
FOR: FL. BAY COASTER CO.
1/4" = 1'-0"   B-28-80
OUTBOARD PROFILE
REV'D.
JAY R. BENFORD
P.O. BOX 447
ST. MICHAELS, MD 21663
(301) 745-3235

20' CLR.

15' WHALER

LADDER UP TO BRIDGEWING

45' FL. BAY COASTER-2
1/4" = 1'-0"   B-28-88
FOR: FL BAY COASTER CO
ACCOMMODATIONS
REV'D. 8-30-88
JAY R. BENFORD
SEATTLE P.O. BOX 447
ST. MICHAELS, MD 21663
(301) 745-3235

SETTEE
DINING TABLE
SEAT
15' WHALER
CARGO HATCH
CHART DRAWERS UNDER

0   5'   10'

DRESSER
HNG. LKR.
WC
SHOWER STALL
FREEZE CHEST
RANGE
SUZUKI SAMURAI
SHOWER STALL
HANGING LKR.
WC
DRESSER
KING SIZE BERTH
HANGING LKR.
SHELVES
DISH WASHER
UP
UP
REFR/FREEZER
DOUBLE BERTH
DRESSER
HNG. LKR.
DECK GEAR LKR.
SHELVES
LANDING

-6 -5 -4 -3 -2 -1 0 1 2 3 4 5 6 7 8 B
24" 36"   36" 12"
270-SP

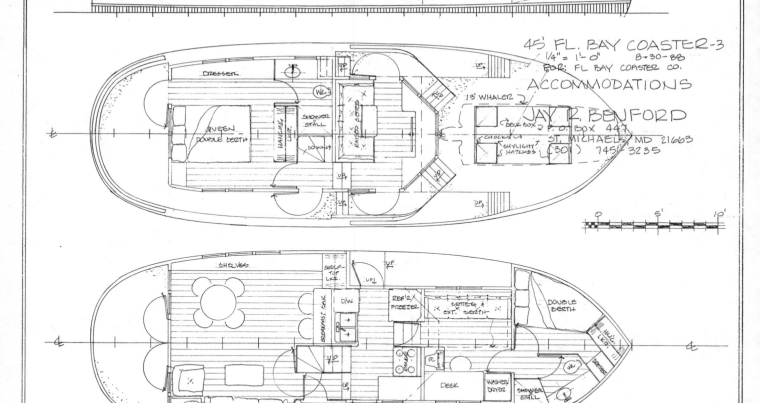

45' FL BAY COASTER-3
FOR: FL BAY COASTER CO.
1/4" = 1'-0"   8/30/88
OUTBOARD PROFILE
REV'D:
JAY R. BENFORD
P.O. BOX 447
ST. MICHAELS, MD 21663
(301) 745-3235

13' WHALER

45' FL. BAY COASTER-3
1/4" = 1'-0"   8-30-88
FOR: FL BAY COASTER CO.
ACCOMMODATIONS
JAY R. BENFORD
P.O. BOX 447
ST. MICHAELS, MD 21663
(301) 745-3235

DRESSER

QUEEN DOUBLE BERTH

SHOWER STALL

HANGING LKR.

RAISED SOLES

DOWN

13' WHALER

DECK BOX

CHOCKS

SKYLIGHT & HATCHES

UP

SHELVES

SHELF-TOP LKR.

D/W.

BREAKFAST BAR

REF'R FREEZER

RANGE

PC

DESK

SETTEE & EXT. BERTH

DOUBLE BERTH

HULL LKR.

DRESSER

WC.

SHOWER STALL

WASHER DRYER

LANDING P/S

WC.

0   5'   10'

5 -6 -5 -4 -3 -2 -1 0 1 2 3 4 5 6 7 8 8
24" 36"   36" 12"
270-7

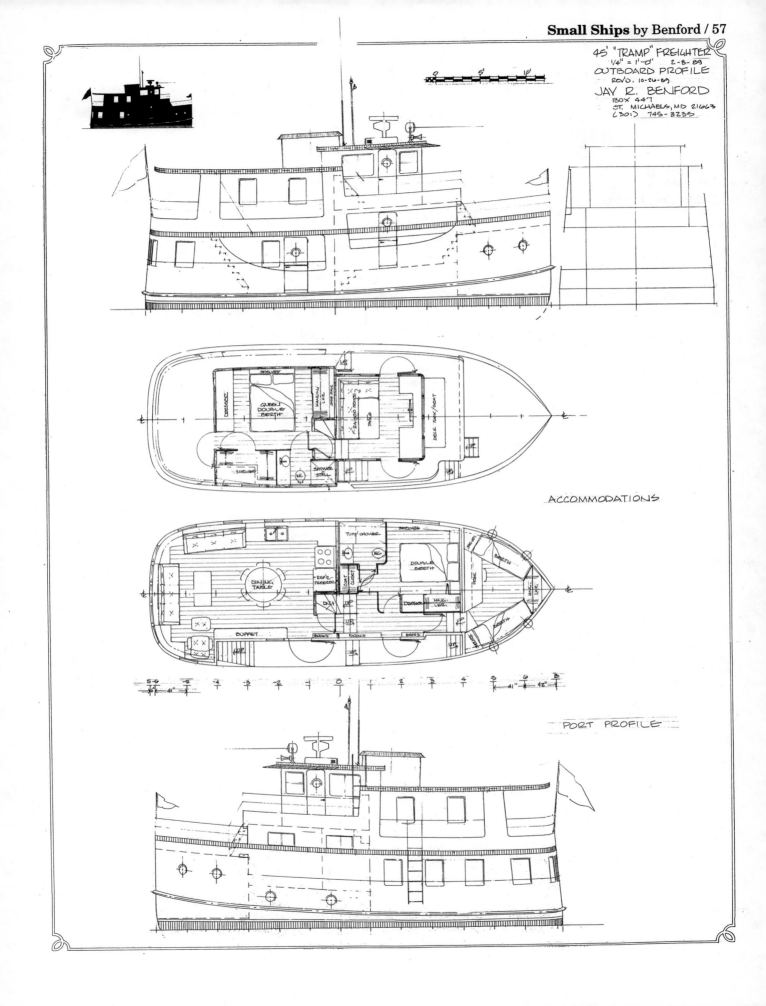

45' "TRAMP" FREIGHTER
1/4" = 1'-0"   2-8-89
OUTBOARD PROFILE
REV'D. 10-26-89
JAY R. BENFORD
BOX 447
ST. MICHAELS, MD 21663
(301) 745-3235

ACCOMMODATIONS

PORT PROFILE

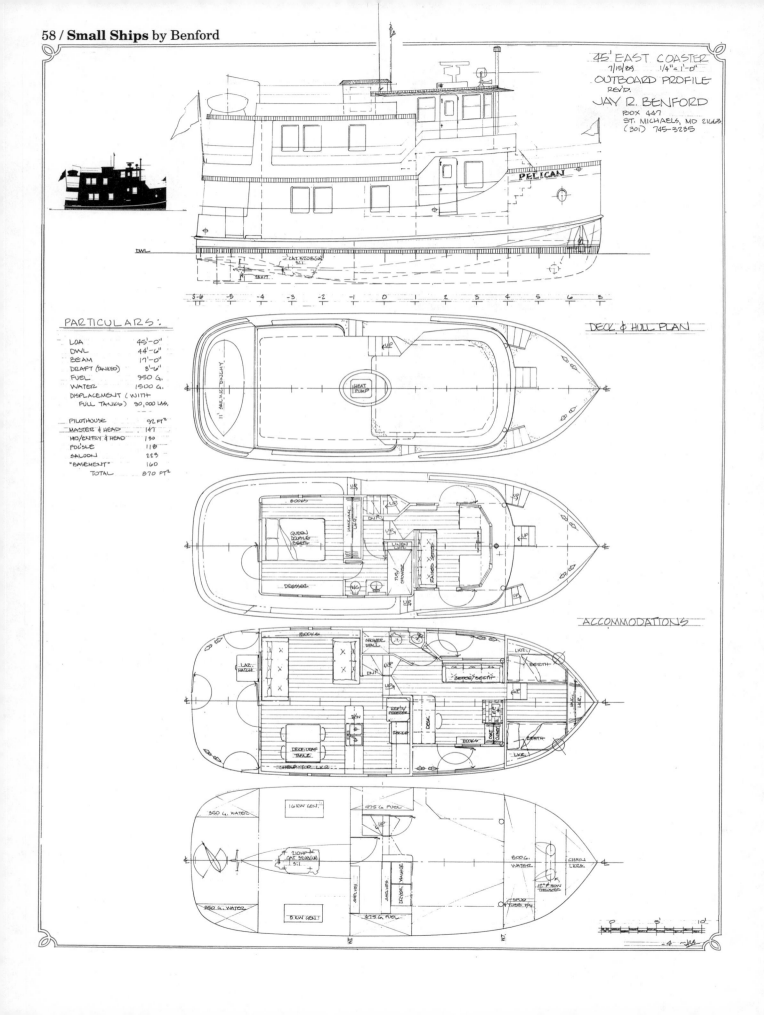

45' EAST COASTER
7/15/89   1/4" = 1'-0"
OUTBOARD PROFILE
REV'D.
JAY R. BENFORD
BOX 447
ST. MICHAELS, MD 21663
(301) 745-3235

DECK & HULL PLAN

PARTICULARS:

LOA	45'-0"
DWL	44'-6"
BEAM	17'-0"
DRAFT (TANKED)	3'-6"
FUEL	950 G.
WATER	1500 G.
DISPLACEMENT (WITH	
FULL TANKS)	90,000 LBS.

PILOTHOUSE	92 FT²
MASTER & HEAD	147
MD/ENTRY & HEAD	130
FO'C'SLE	118
SALOON	223
"BASEMENT"	160
TOTAL	870 FT²

ACCOMMODATIONS

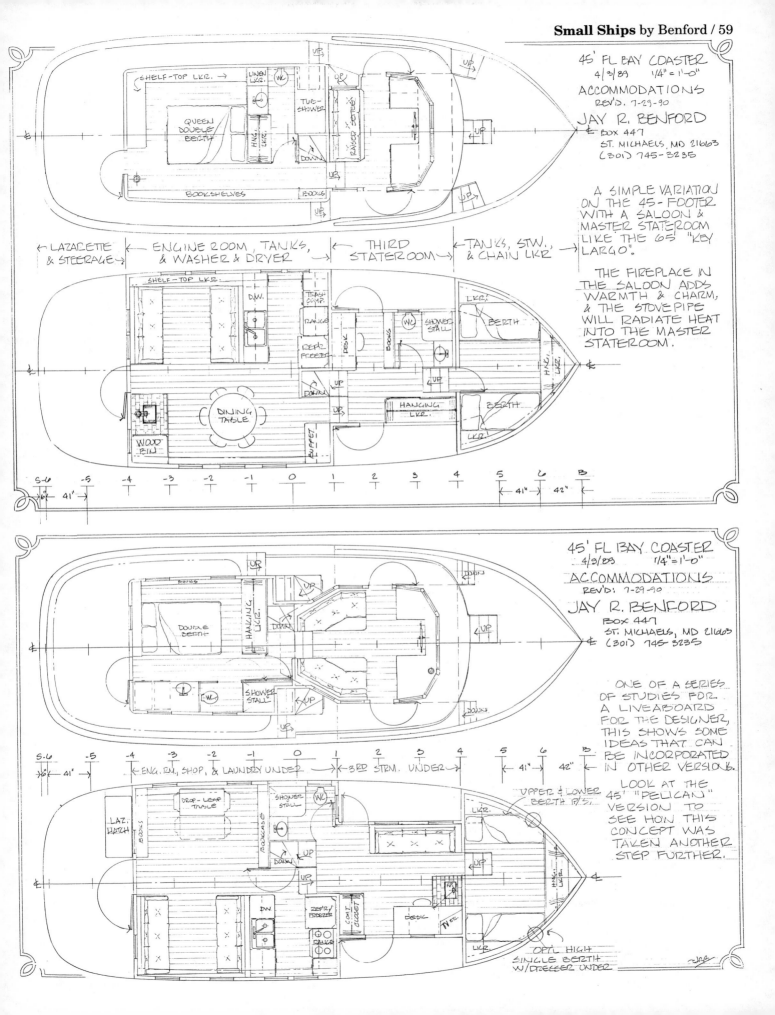

45' FL BAY COASTER
4/3/89   1/4" = 1'-0"
ACCOMMODATIONS
REV'D. 7-29-90
JAY R. BENFORD
BOX 447
ST. MICHAELS, MD 21663
(301) 745-3235

A SIMPLE VARIATION ON THE 45-FOOTER WITH A SALOON & MASTER STATEROOM LIKE THE 65' "KEY LARGO".

THE FIREPLACE IN THE SALOON ADDS WARMTH & CHARM, & THE STOVEPIPE WILL RADIATE HEAT INTO THE MASTER STATEROOM.

← LAZARETTE & STEERAGE →   ← ENGINE ROOM, TANKS, & WASHER & DRYER →   ← THIRD STATEROOM →   ← TANKS, STW., & CHAIN LKR. →

45' FL BAY COASTER
4/3/89   1/4" = 1'-0"
ACCOMMODATIONS
REV'D: 7-29-90
JAY R. BENFORD
BOX 447
ST. MICHAELS, MD 21663
(301) 745-3235

ONE OF A SERIES OF STUDIES FOR A LIVEABOARD FOR THE DESIGNER, THIS SHOWS SOME IDEAS THAT CAN BE INCORPORATED IN OTHER VERSIONS.

LOOK AT THE 45' "PELICAN" VERSION TO SEE HOW THIS CONCEPT WAS TAKEN ANOTHER STEP FURTHER.

← ENG. RM., SHOP, & LAUNDRY UNDER →   ← 3RD STRM. UNDER →

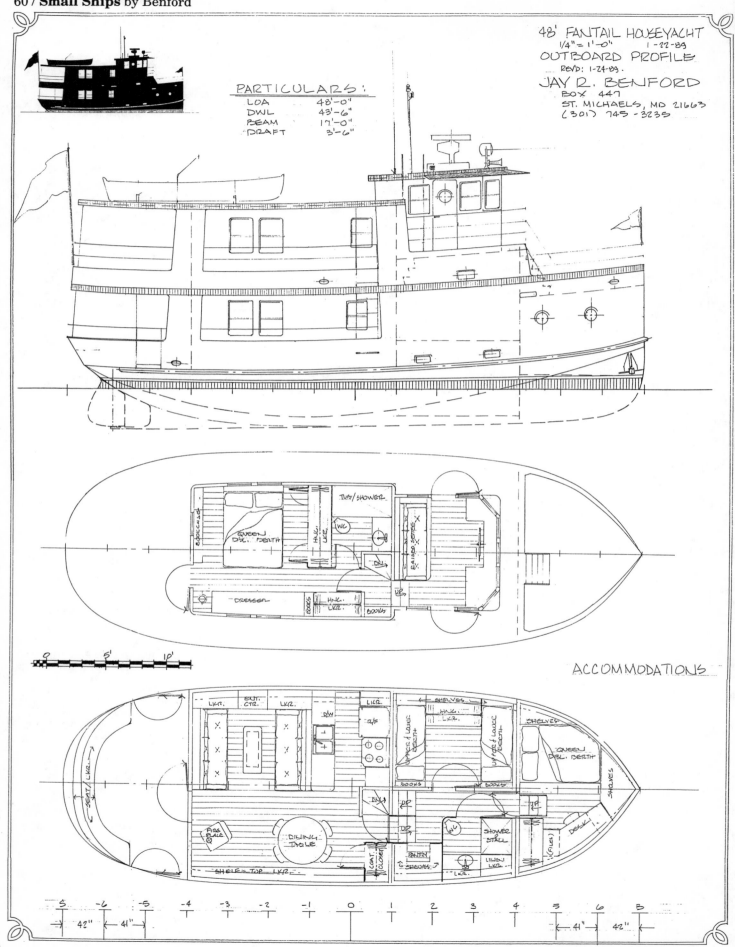

48' FANTAIL HOUSEYACHT
1/4"=1'-0"   1-22-89
OUTBOARD PROFILE
REVD: 1-24-89.

JAY R. BENFORD
BOX 447
ST. MICHAELS, MD 21663
(301) 745-3235

PARTICULARS:
LOA   48'-0"
DWL   43'-6"
BEAM   17'-0"
DRAFT   3'-6"

ACCOMMODATIONS

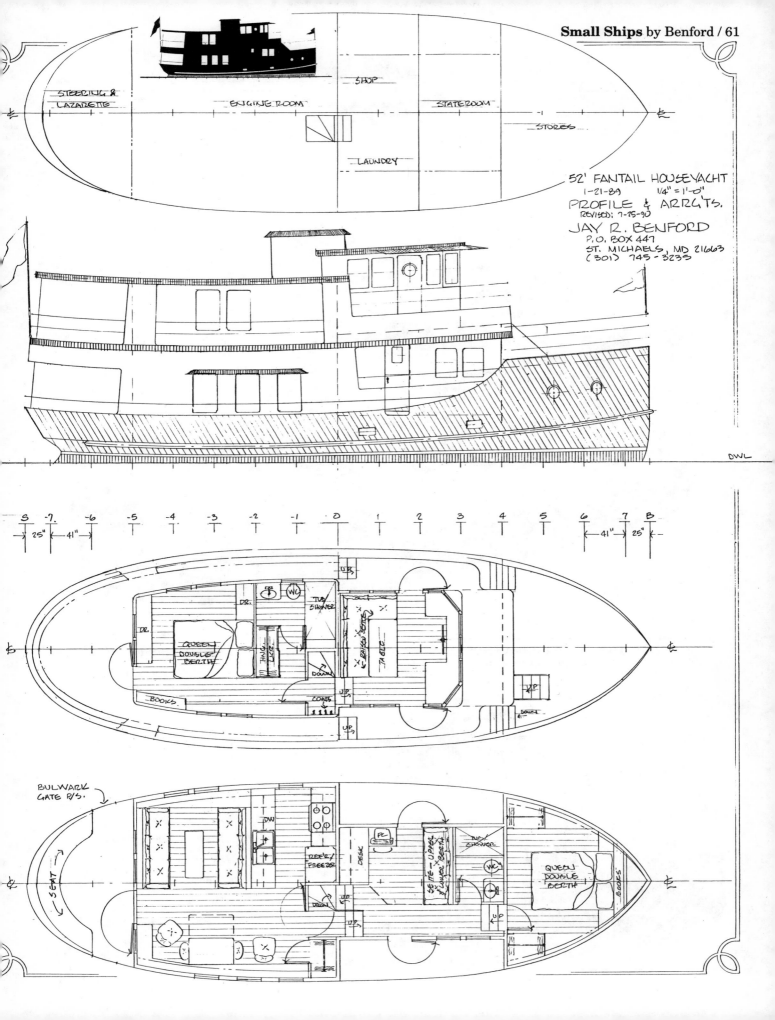

STEERING & LAZARETTE

ENGINE ROOM

SHOP

STATEROOM

STORES

LAUNDRY

52' FANTAIL HOUSEYACHT
1-21-89   1/4" = 1'-0"
PROFILE & ARRG'TS.
REVISED: 7-25-90
JAY R. BENFORD
P.O. BOX 447
ST. MICHAELS, MD 21663
(301) 745-3235

DWL

S   -7   -6   -5   -4   -3   -2   -1   0   1   2   3   4   5   6   7   B
25"   41"   41"   25"

QUEEN DOUBLE BERTH

DR.

WC

TUB SHOWER

RAISED SEAT

TABLE

DOWN

COATS

BOOKS

UP

UP

DOWN

BULWARK GATE P/S.

SEAT

DW

REEF'Y/FREEZER

DESK

PL

SETTEE - UPPER & LOWER BERTH

TUB SHOWER

WC

QUEEN DOUBLE BERTH

BOOKS

DOWN

UP

UP

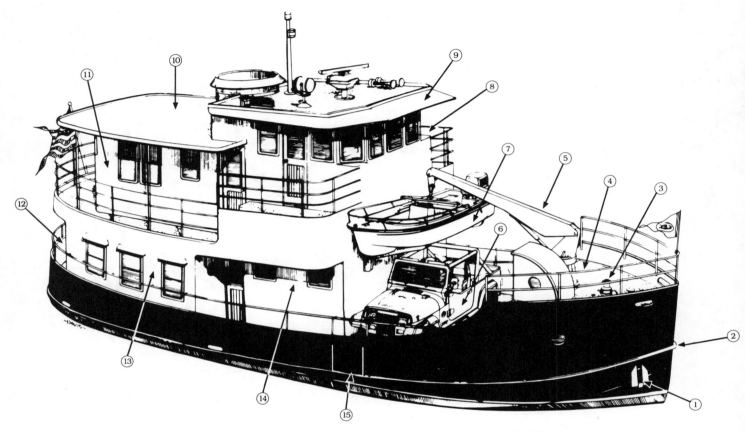

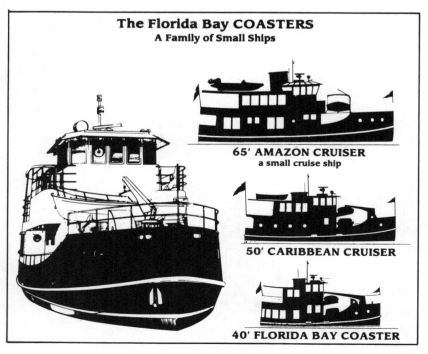

The Florida Bay COASTERS
A Family of Small Ships

65' AMAZON CRUISER
a small cruise ship

50' CARIBBEAN CRUISER

40' FLORIDA BAY COASTER

1. Self-stowing anchor

2. 4" rubber rubrail

3. Reversible anchor windlass

4. Raised foc'sle deck

5. 3500# crane (optional)

6. Jeep® (optional)

7. 14' launch on cradle (optional)

8. Wings (port & starboard)

9. Pilot house

10. Boat deck

11. Raised master stateroom

12. Covered rear deck

13. Main saloon

14. Mid deck guest and head

15. Bulwark gate (port & starboard)

50' FLORIDA BAY & 65' KEY LARGO

The 50' FLORIDA BAY was the first in this series of our freighter designs to be built. She generated tremendous enthusiasm amongst all those who saw her, and in her builder and designer too. This excitement led to the series of drawings that follows, as we explored a variety of uses for variations of her.

Questions about her stability were put to rest with demonstrations of how still she was with the Jeep hanging over the side of the crane. She heeled only about three degrees. At sea, she felt very powerful, like a large freighter, with very little heeling. We did an inclining test when we launched her, confirming our calculations of her great stability. At anchor, most wakes just bounced off her and weren't noticed.

The second 50-footer, under construction for fall 1990 delivery, has a layout like the 45' SAILS, with an additional stateroom or study added. Like SAILS, she has a combination workshop and laundry room under the galley, with easy access to the engine room. She is shown on page 66.

The 65' KEY LARGO was the next freighter built by Florida Bay Coaster Company. In her, we took the opportunity to try out all the ideas for improvements we'd generated in using the 50-footer. All her cabins are larger, she has luxury additions like the skylight over the master stateroom and the hot tub on deck in place of the stack, full headroom in the hold area, opening up options like a captain's cabin in this space, and greatly increased tankage and a watermaker, making possible extended time away from shore.

Florida Bay Coaster Company has put out some excellent descriptive literature and a VHS video of the boats in use. Drop us a line or give us a call and we'll put you in touch with them.

The first loading of the JEEP. Note the small angle of heel with this large weight suspended well outboard.

The widely spaced props make for wonderful maneouverability. The props are well protected with struts to the hull and back under the rudders, making for "no problems" groundings while exploring or off-loading the JEEP.

The COASTER was "walked" from the building shed to the water, just shy of four months from laying the keel, for her launching. She sat comfortably on her keel and skegs. The lifting was done on her mooring cleats and stem, a testament to the ruggedness of her structure.

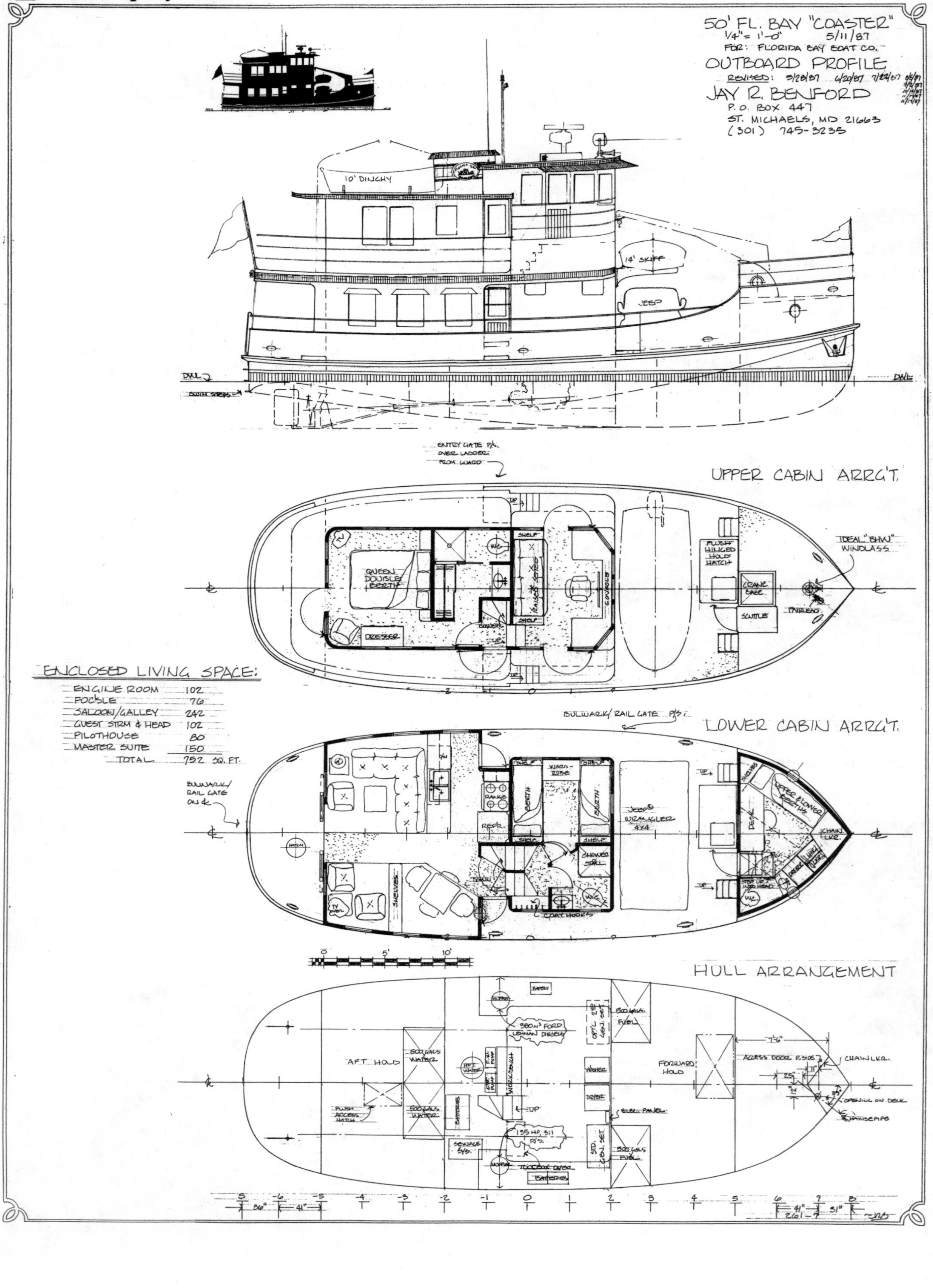

50' FL. BAY "COASTER"
1/4" = 1'-0" 5/11/87
FOR: FLORIDA BAY BOAT CO.
OUTBOARD PROFILE
REVISED: 5/28/87 6/20/87 7/22/87
JAY R. BENFORD
P. O. BOX 447
ST. MICHAELS, MD 21663
(301) 745-3235
10' DINGHY
14' SKIFF
JEEP
DWL
SWIM STEPS
ENTRY GATE P/S OVER LADDER FROM GUARD
UPPER CABIN ARRG'T.
QUEEN DOUBLE BERTH
DRESSER
SHELF
W.C.
RAISED SETTEE
CONSOLE
FLUSH HINGED HOLD HATCH
CRANE BASE
SCUTTLE
FAIRLEAD
IDEAL "BHW" WINDLASS
ENCLOSED LIVING SPACE:
ENGINE ROOM 102
FOC'SLE 76
SALOON/GALLEY 242
GUEST STRM & HEAD 102
PILOTHOUSE 80
MASTER SUITE 150
TOTAL 752 SQ. FT.
BULWARK/RAIL GATE P/S
LOWER CABIN ARRG'T.
BULWARK/RAIL GATE ON ℄
HATCH
SHELVES
RANGE
REFR.
BERTH
WARDROBE
SHOWER STALL
COATHOOKS
JEEP WRANGLER 4X4
UPPER & LOWER BERTHS
DESK
CHAIN LKR.
0 5' 10'
HULL ARRANGEMENT
AFT HOLD
500 GALS WATER
HOT WATER
WORKBENCH
BATTERIES
FLUSH ACCESS HATCH
SEWAGE
UP
135 HP, 3:1 P/S
TOOLBOX OVER BATTERIES
380 HP FORD LEHMAN DIESEL
OPT'L 2ND GEN. SET
500 GALS FUEL
WASHER
DRYER
ELEC. PANEL
STD. GEN. SET
FORWARD HOLD
ACCESS DOOR P. SIDE
CHAIN LKR.
OPENING ON DECK
HAWSEPIPE

ENCLOSED LIVING SPACE:

ENGINE ROOM	102
FOC'SLE	76
SALOON/GALLEY	242
GUEST STRM & HEAD	102
PILOTHOUSE	80
MASTER SUITE	178
TOTAL	780 SQ. FT.

NOTE: MASTER STATEROOM EXPANDED WITH EXTERIOR WALLS FOLLOWING SHEER, GIVING ROOM FOR BATHTUB AND BOOKCASE.

50' FL. BAY "COASTER"
1/4" = 1'-0"   11/28/07
FOR: FLORIDA BAY BOAT CO.
UPPER CABIN — ALT. A

JAY R. BENFORD
P.O. BOX 447
ST. MICHAELS, MD 21663
(301) 745-3235

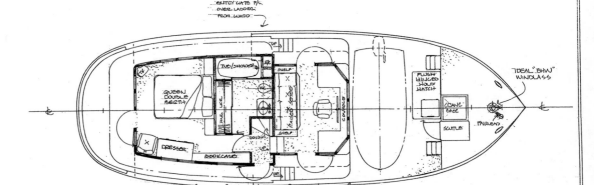

ENCLOSED LIVING SPACE:

ENGINE ROOM	102
FOC'SLE	76
SALOON/GALLEY	242
GUEST STRM & HEAD	102
PILOTHOUSE	80
MASTER SUITE	208
TOTAL	810 SQ. FT.

NOTE: MASTER STATEROOM EXTENDED TO DECK EDGE ON PORT SIDE ONLY.

UPPER CABIN — ALT. B

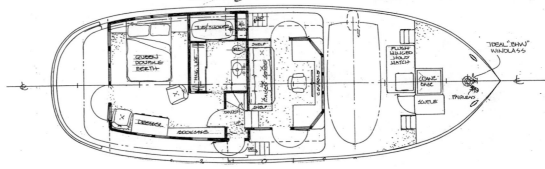

ENCLOSED LIVING SPACE:

ENGINE ROOM	102
FOC'SLE	76
SALOON/GALLEY	242
GUEST STRM & HEAD	102
PILOTHOUSE	80
MASTER SUITE	238
TOTAL	840 SQ.FT.

NOTE: MASTER STATEROOM EXTENDED TO DECK EDGE PORT AND STARBOARD, AND OFFICE INCLUDED IN CORNER.

UPPER CABIN — ALT. C

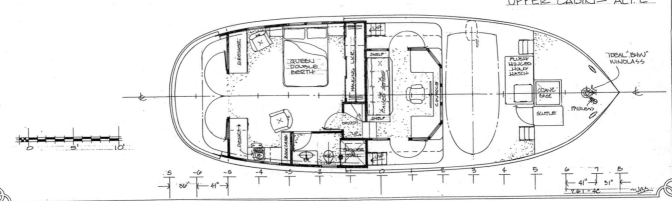

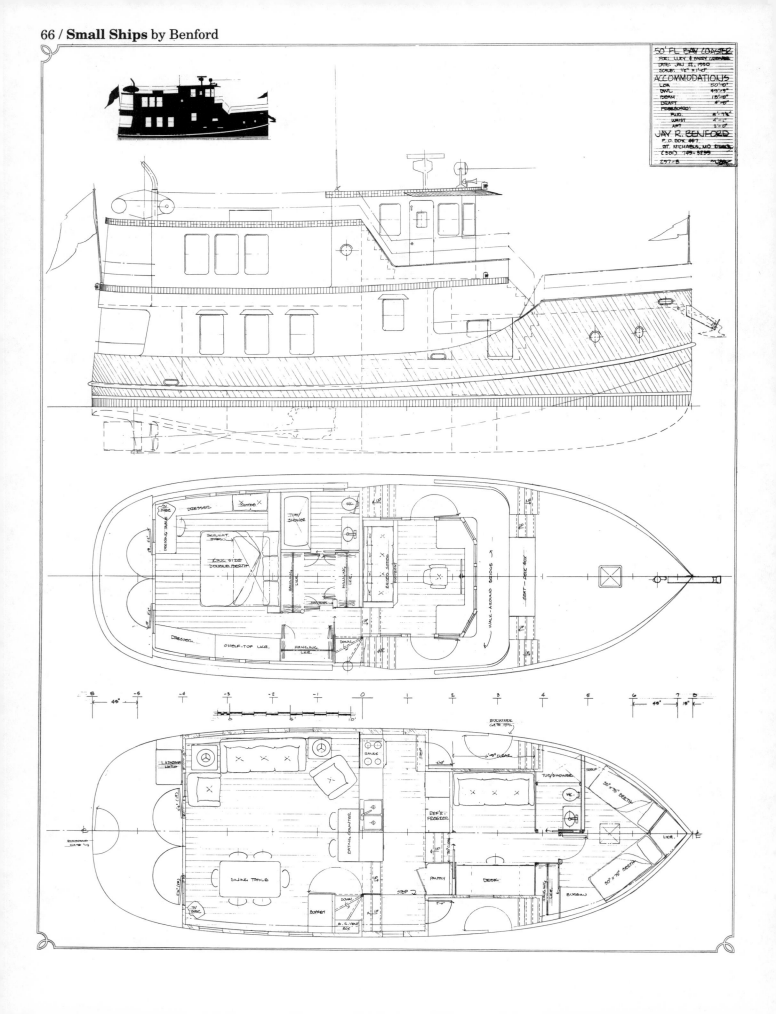

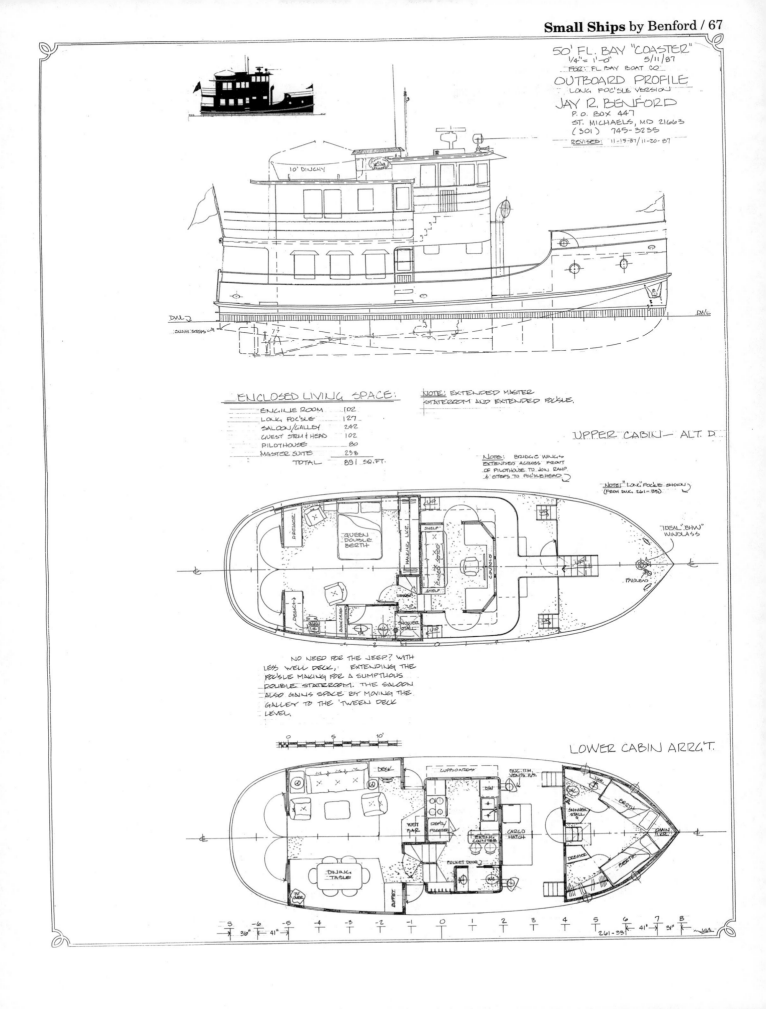

50' FL. BAY "COASTER"
1/4" = 1'-0"   5/11/87
FOR FL BAY BOAT CO.
OUTBOARD PROFILE
LONG FOC'SLE VERSION
JAY R. BENFORD
P. O. BOX 447
ST. MICHAELS, MD 21663
(301) 745-3235
REVISED: 11-19-87/11-20-87

10' DINGHY

DWL

SWIM STEPS

ENCLOSED LIVING SPACE:

ENGINE ROOM	102
LONG FOC'SLE	127
SALOON/GALLEY	242
GUEST STRM & HEAD	102
PILOTHOUSE	80
MASTER SUITE	238
TOTAL	891 SQ.FT.

NOTE: EXTENDED MASTER
STATEROOM AND EXTENDED FOC'SLE.

UPPER CABIN — ALT. D

NOTE: BRIDGE WINGS
EXTENDED ACROSS FRONT
OF PILOTHOUSE TO JON RAMP
& STEPS TO FOC'SLEHEAD

NOTE: "LONG" FOC'SLE SHOWN)
(FROM DWG. 261-35)

"IDEAL "BHW"
WINDLASS

DRESSER

QUEEN
DOUBLE
BERTH

SHELF

HANGING LKR.

DESK

SHELF

CONTROLS

UP

FAIRLEAD

NO NEED FOR THE JEEP? WITH
LESS WELL DECK, EXTENDING THE
FOC'SLE MAKING FOR A SUMPTUOUS
DOUBLE STATEROOM. THE SALOON
ALSO GAINS SPACE BY MOVING THE
GALLEY TO THE 'TWEEN DECK
LEVEL.

0   5   10'

LOWER CABIN ARR'G'T.

DESK

CUPBOARDS

ENG. RM.
VENTS P/S.

WET
BAR

DW

DEEP
FREEZER

EATING
COUNTER

CARGO
HATCH

SHOWER
STALL

BERTH

CHAIN
LKR.

POCKET DOOR

WC

DRESSER

BERTH

DINING
TABLE

TV OVER

BUFFET

-8   -6   -5   -4   -3   -2   -1   0   1   2   3   4   5   6   7   8
36"   41"   261-35   41"   31"

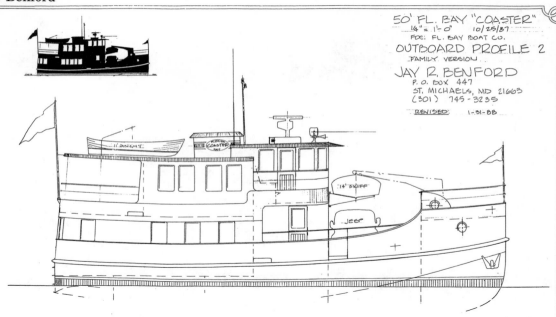

50' FL. BAY "COASTER"
¼" = 1'-0"   10/25/87
FOR: FL. BAY BOAT CO.
OUTBOARD PROFILE 2
FAMILY VERSION
JAY R. BENFORD
P.O. BOX 447
ST. MICHAELS, MD 21663
(301) 745-3235
REVISED: 1-31-88

NOTE: THE FULL WIDTH SALOON
AND GALLEY ENJOY THE ELEVATED
VIEW AVAILABLE ON THE UPPER
DECK. THE LARGER AFTER DECK
MAKES UP FOR NOT HAVING ONE ON
THE LOWER LEVEL.

UPPER CABIN ARR'G'T. 2

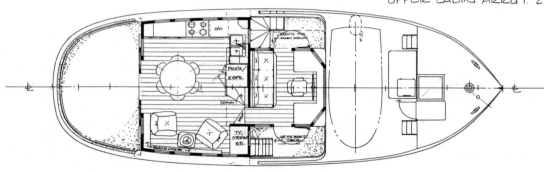

NOTE: THE FAMILY VERSION OF THE 50
HAS THREE STATEROOMS AFT PLUS ONE
IN THE FOC'SLE. THE MASTER STATEROOM
AFT HAS ITS OWN HEAD, AND THE TWO
SMALLER ONES (FOR THE KIDS) SHARE
THE HEAD IN THE PASSAGEWAY.

THE FOC'SLE SHOWN HERE GIVES
A LARGER HEAD, WITH SEPARATE
SHOWER STALL, THAN ON THE STANDARD
50.

LOWER CABIN ARR'G'T 2

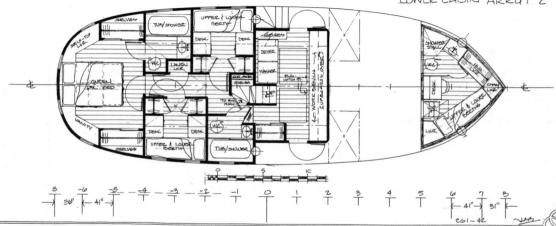

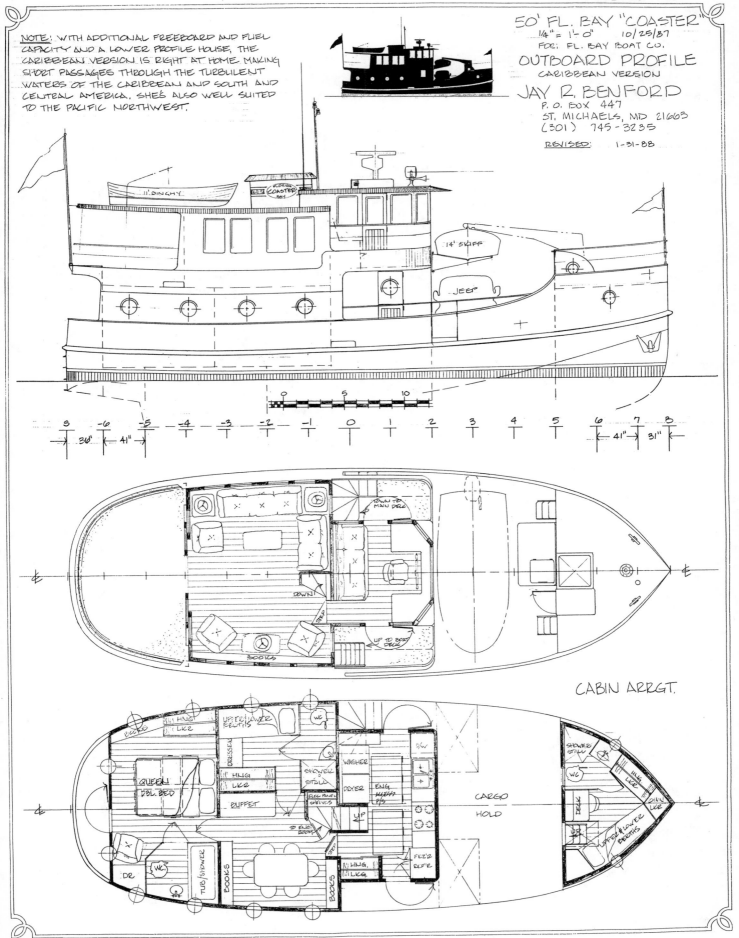

NOTE: WITH ADDITIONAL FREEBOARD AND FUEL CAPACITY AND A LOWER PROFILE HOUSE, THE CARIBBEAN VERSION IS RIGHT AT HOME MAKING SHORT PASSAGES THROUGH THE TURBULENT WATERS OF THE CARIBBEAN AND SOUTH AND CENTRAL AMERICA. SHE'S ALSO WELL SUITED TO THE PACIFIC NORTHWEST.

50' FL. BAY "COASTER"
1/4" = 1'-0"   10/25/87
FOR: FL. BAY BOAT CO.
OUTBOARD PROFILE
CARIBBEAN VERSION
JAY R. BENFORD
P. O. BOX 447
ST. MICHAELS, MD 21663
(301) 745-3235
REVISED: 1-31-88

11' DINGHY

FLORIDA COASTER BAY

14' SKIFF

JEEP

CABIN ARRGT.

QUEEN DBL. BED

CARGO HOLD

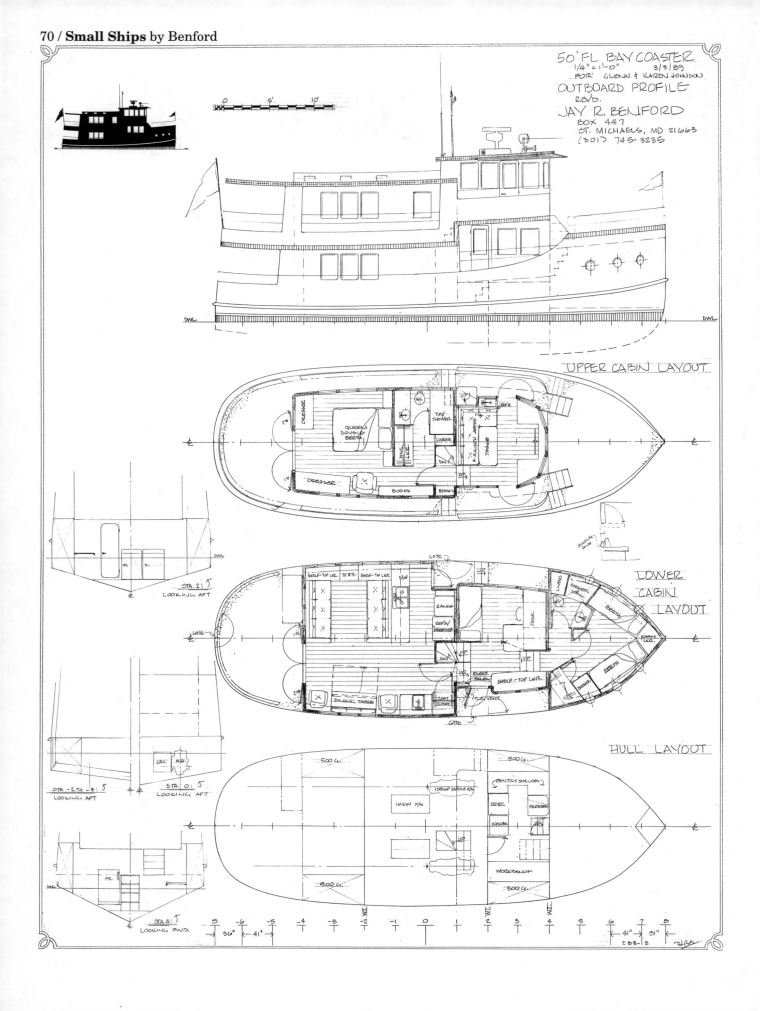

50' FL BAY COASTER
1/4" = 1'-0"   3/3/89
FOR: GLENN & KAREN JOHNSON

OUTBOARD PROFILE
REVD.

JAY R. BENFORD
BOX 447
ST. MICHAELS, MD 21663
(301) 745-3235

UPPER CABIN LAYOUT

LOWER CABIN LAYOUT

HULL LAYOUT

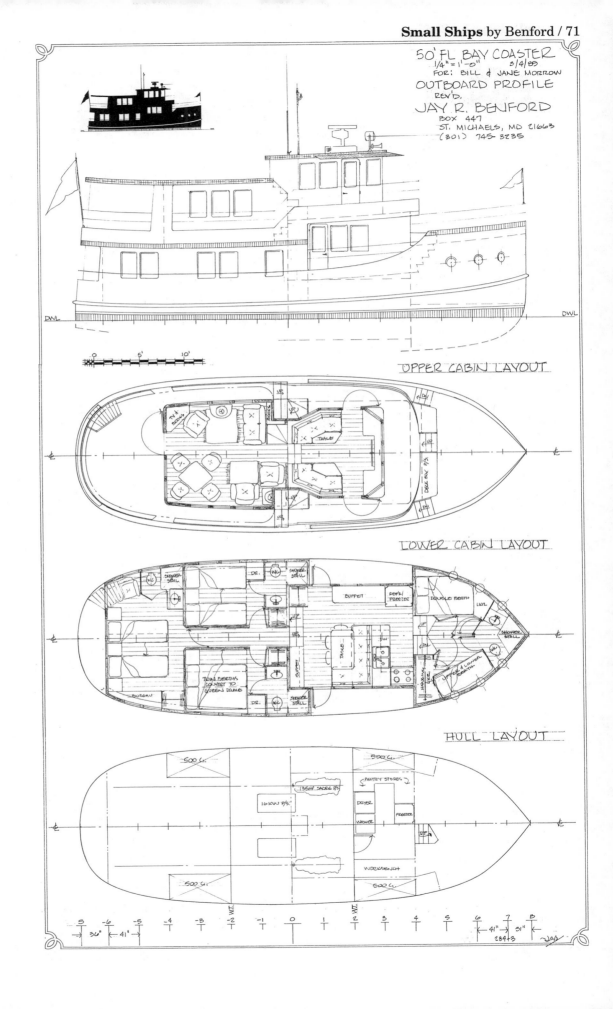

50' FL BAY COASTER
1/4" = 1'-0"   5/4/89
FOR: BILL & JANE MORROW
OUTBOARD PROFILE
REV'd.
JAY R. BENFORD
BOX 447
ST. MICHAELS, MD 21663
(301) 745-3235

UPPER CABIN LAYOUT

LOWER CABIN LAYOUT

HULL LAYOUT

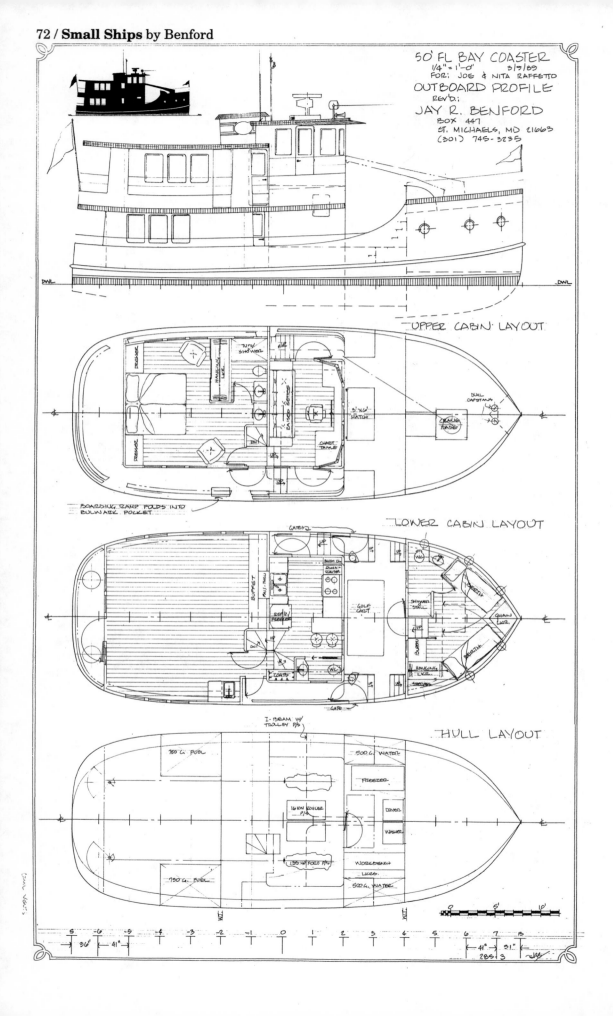

50' FL BAY COASTER
1/4" = 1'-0"   3/9/89
FOR: JOE & NITA RAFFETTO
OUTBOARD PROFILE
REV'D:
JAY R. BENFORD
BOX 447
ST. MICHAELS, MD 21663
(301) 745-3235

UPPER CABIN LAYOUT

LOWER CABIN LAYOUT

HULL LAYOUT

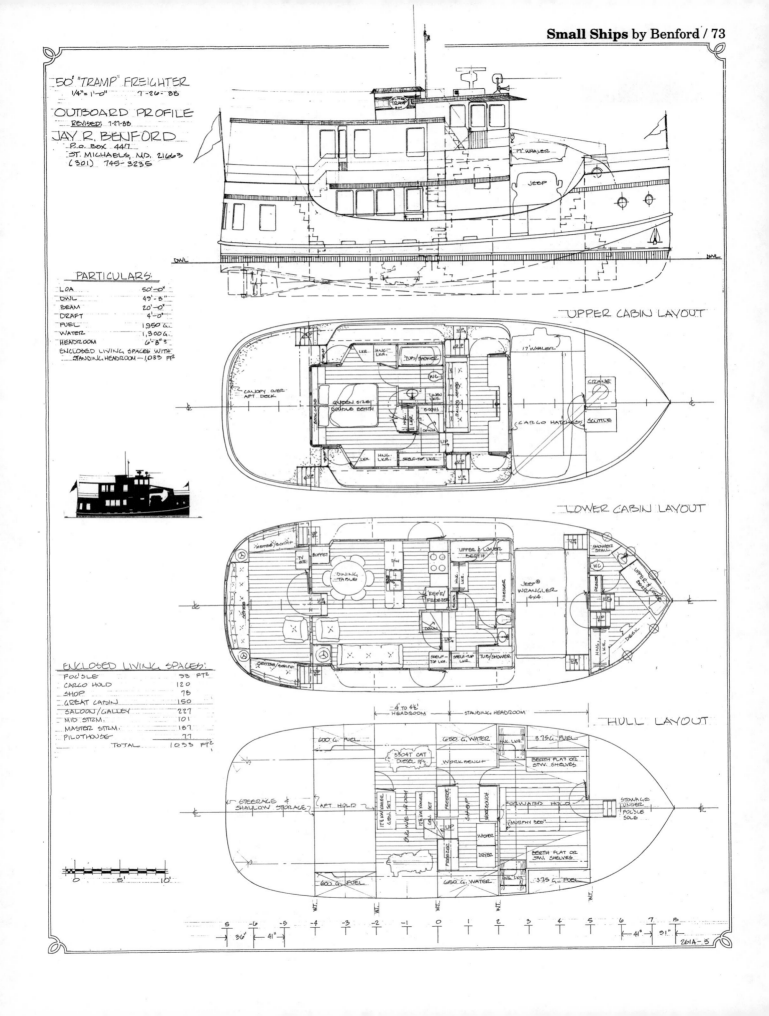

50' "TRAMP" FREIGHTER
1/4"=1'-0"   7-26-88

OUTBOARD PROFILE
REVISED: 1-27-88

JAY R. BENFORD
P.O. BOX 447
ST. MICHAELS, MD. 21663
(301) 745-3235

PARTICULARS:

LOA	50'-0"
DWL	49'-8"
BEAM	20'-0"
DRAFT	4'-0"
FUEL	1,950 G.
WATER	1,300 G.
HEADROOM	6'-8" ±

ENCLOSED LIVING SPACES WITH
STANDING HEADROOM — 1,033 FT²

UPPER CABIN LAYOUT

LOWER CABIN LAYOUT

ENCLOSED LIVING SPACES:

FO'C'SLE	93 FT²
CARGO HOLD	120
SHOP	78
GREAT CABIN	150
SALOON/GALLEY	227
MID STRM.	101
MASTER STRM.	187
PILOTHOUSE	77
TOTAL	1033 FT²

HULL LAYOUT

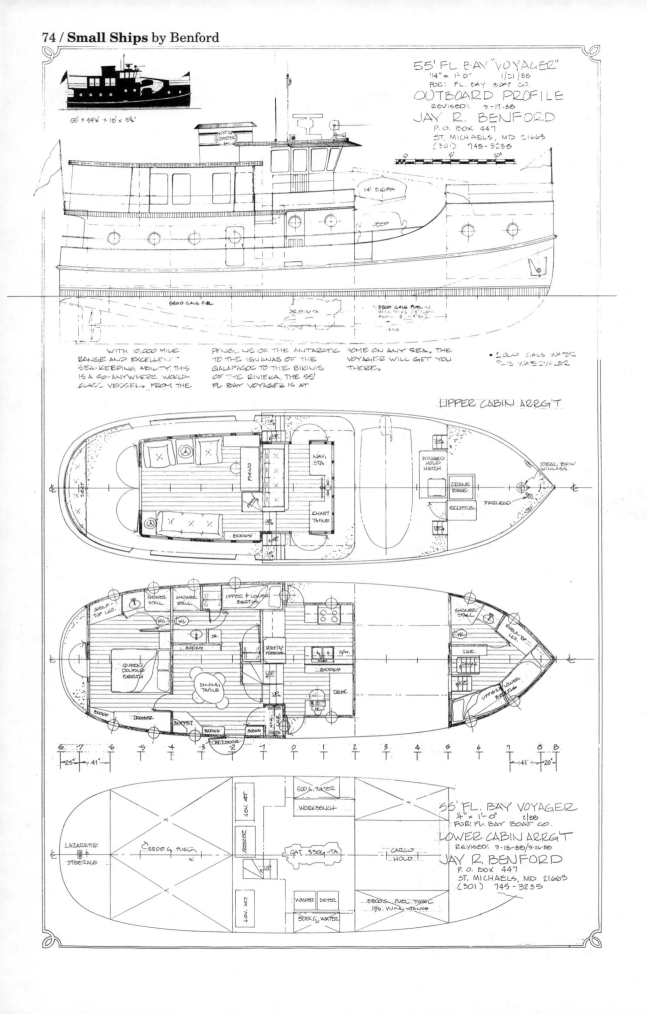

55' × 54'6" × 13' × 5½'

55' FL BAY "VOYAGER"
¼" = 1'-0"   1/21/88
FOR: FL. BAY CO.
OUTBOARD PROFILE
REVISED: 9-17-88
JAY R. BENFORD
P.O. BOX 447
ST. MICHAELS, MD 21663
(301) 745-3235

WITH 10,000 MILE RANGE AND EXCELLENT SEA-KEEPING ABILITY, THIS IS A GO-ANYWHERE WORLD-CLASS VESSEL. FROM THE PENGUINS OF THE ANTARCTIC TO THE IGUANAS OF THE GALAPAGOS TO THE BIKINIS OF THE RIVIERA, THE 55' FL BAY VOYAGER IS AT HOME ON ANY SEA, THE VOYAGER WILL GET YOU THERE.

UPPER CABIN ARR'G'T

55' FL. BAY VOYAGER
¼" = 1'-0"   2/88
FOR: FL. BAY BOAT CO.
LOWER CABIN ARR'G'T
REVISED: 9-18-88/9-26-88
JAY R. BENFORD
P.O. BOX 447
ST. MICHAELS, MD 21663
(301) 745-3235

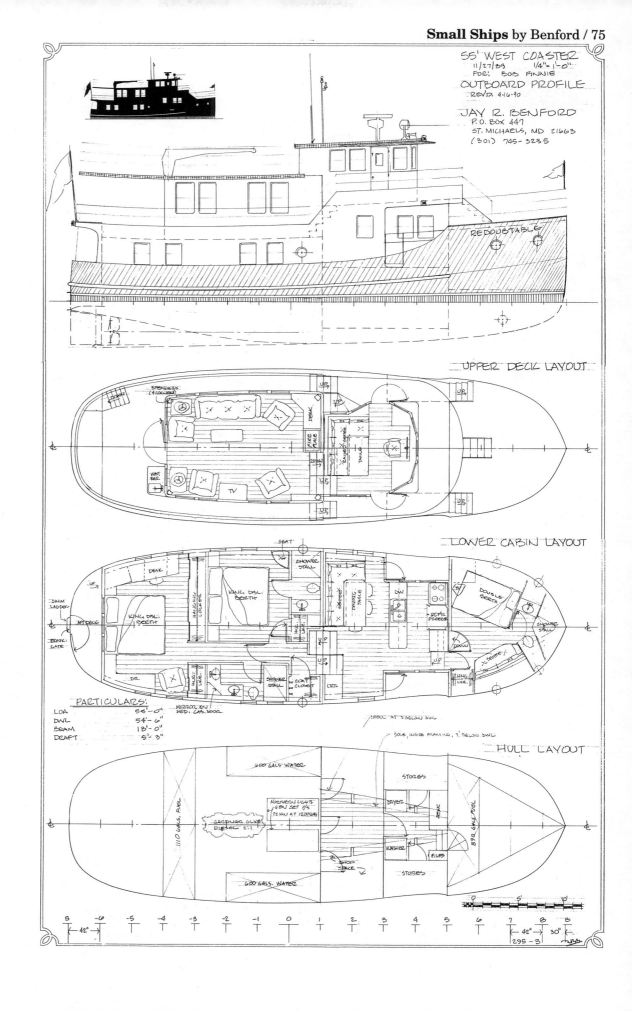

55' WEST COASTER
11/27/89   1/4"=1'-0"
FOR: BOB FINNIE
OUTBOARD PROFILE
REV'D 4-16-90

JAY R. BENFORD
P.O. BOX 447
ST. MICHAELS, MD 21663
(301) 745-3235

REDOUBTABLE

UPPER DECK LAYOUT

LOWER CABIN LAYOUT

PARTICULARS:
LOA   55'-0"
DWL   54'-6"
BEAM   18'-0"
DRAFT   5'-3"

HULL LAYOUT

600 GALS WATER
STORES
NORTHERN LIGHTS
14 KW SET P/S
22 KW AT 1200 RPM
GARDNER 6LXB
DIESEL 2:1
DRYER
DESK
1110 GALS FUEL
WASHER
FILES
892 GALS FUEL
STORES
600 GALS. WATER
STORES

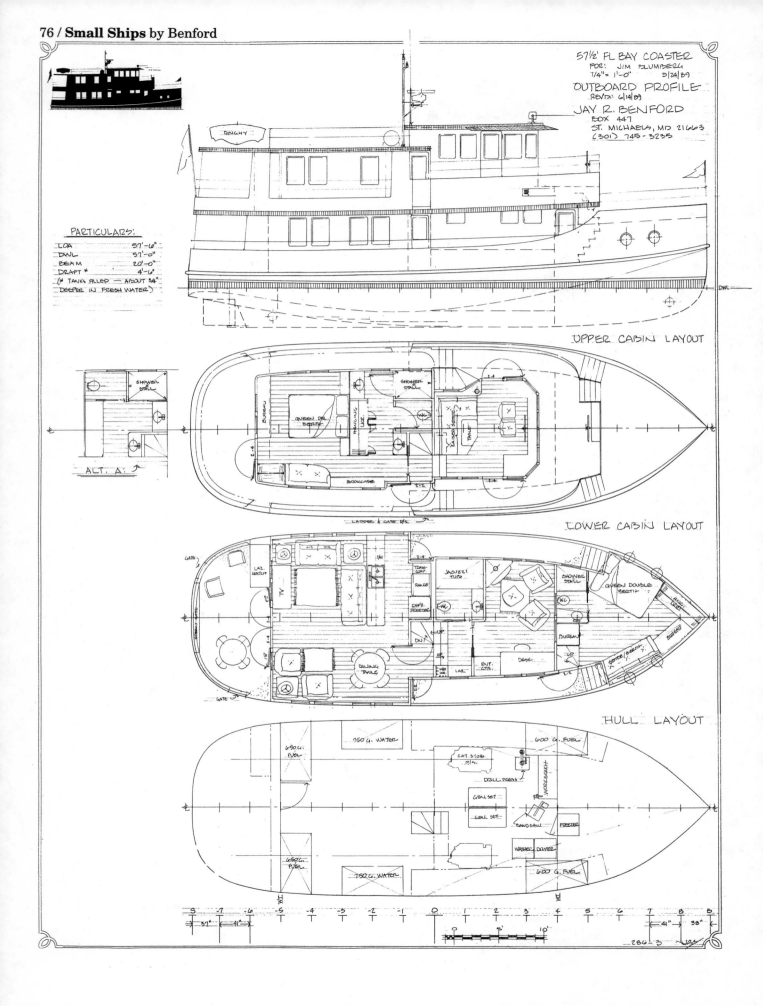

57½' FL BAY COASTER
FOR: JIM PLUMBERG
1/4" = 1'-0"   5/24/89

OUTBOARD PROFILE
REVISED: 6/14/89

JAY R. BENFORD
BOX 447
ST. MICHAELS, MD 21663
(301) 745-3235

PARTICULARS:
LOA   57'-6"
DWL   57'-0"
BEAM   20'-0"
DRAFT *   4'-6"
(* TANKS FILLED — ABOUT 54"
DEEPER IN FRESH WATER)

ALT. "A"

UPPER CABIN LAYOUT

LOWER CABIN LAYOUT

HULL LAYOUT

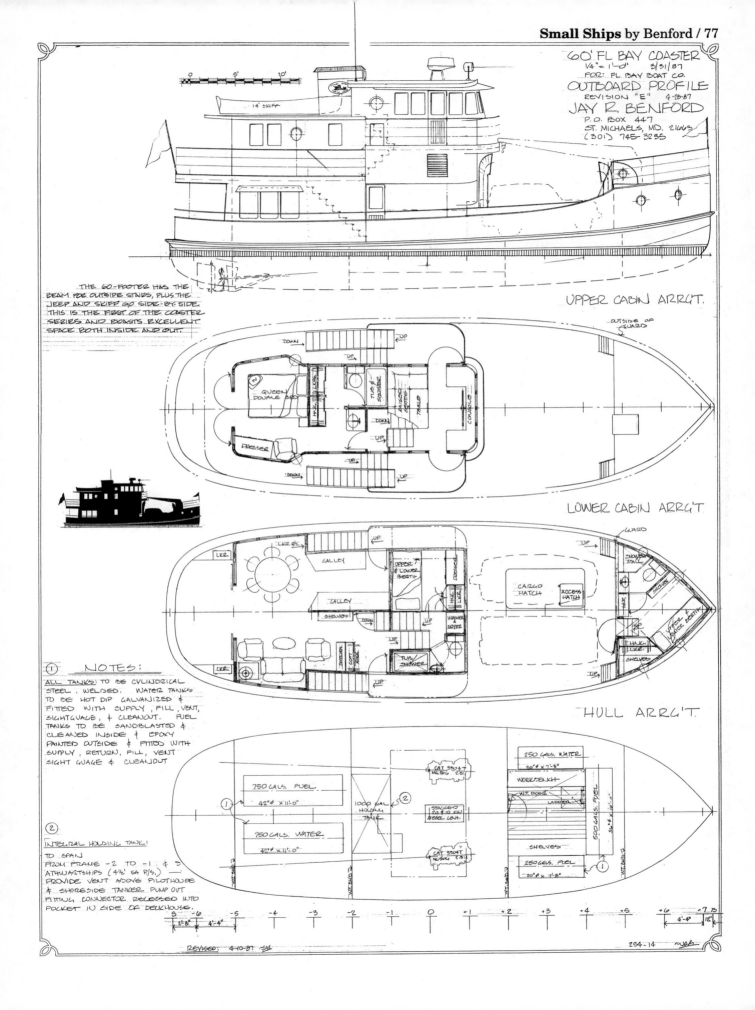

60' FL BAY COASTER
1/4"=1'-0"   3/31/87
FOR: FL BAY BOAT CO.
OUTBOARD PROFILE
REVISION "E"   4-28-87
JAY R. BENFORD
P.O. BOX 447
ST. MICHAELS, MD. 21663
(301) 745-3235

THE 60-FOOTER HAS THE
BEAM FOR OUTSIDE STAIRS, PLUS THE
JEEP AND SKIFF GO SIDE-BY-SIDE.
THIS IS THE FIRST OF THE COASTER
SERIES AND BOASTS EXCELLENT
SPACE BOTH INSIDE AND OUT.

UPPER CABIN ARRG'T.

LOWER CABIN ARRG'T

HULL ARRG'T.

① ___ NOTES:

ALL TANKS: TO BE CYLINDRICAL
STEEL, WELDED. WATER TANKS
TO BE HOT DIP GALVANIZED &
FITTED WITH SUPPLY, FILL, VENT,
SIGHTGUAGE, & CLEANOUT. FUEL
TANKS TO BE SANDBLASTED &
CLEANED INSIDE & EPOXY
PAINTED OUTSIDE & FITTED WITH
SUPPLY, RETURN, FILL, VENT
SIGHT GUAGE & CLEANOUT

② ___

INTEGRAL HOLDING TANK:
TO SPAN
FROM FRAME -2 TO -1, & 5
ATHWARTSHIPS (4½' EA P/S.) —
PROVIDE VENT ABOVE PILOTHOUSE
& SHORESIDE TANKER PUMP OUT
FITTING CONNECTOR RECESSED INTO
POCKET IN SIDE OF DECKHOUSE.

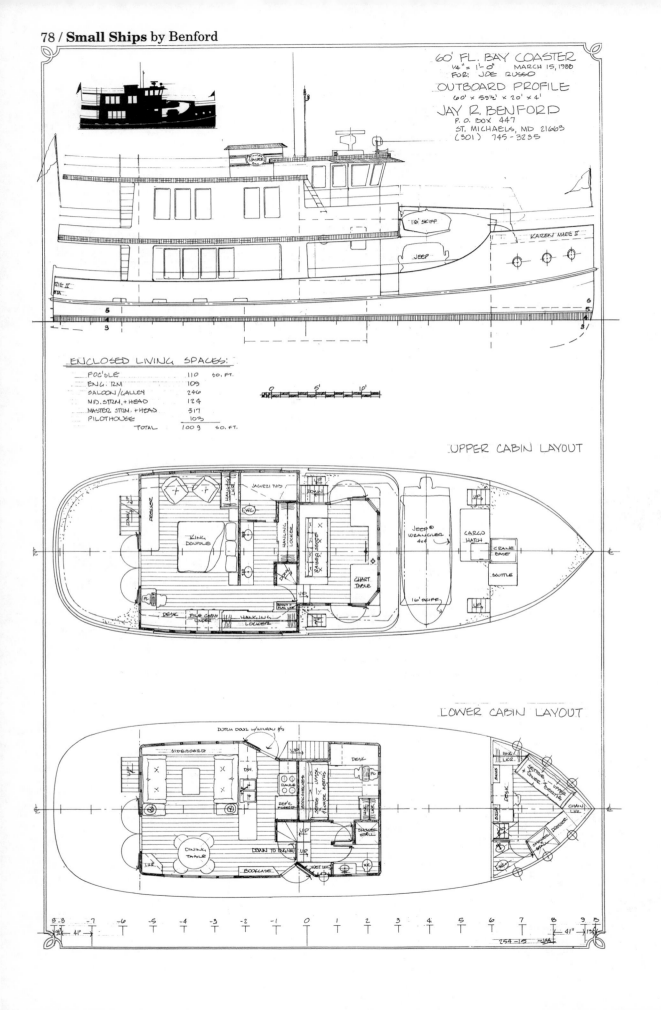

60' FL. BAY COASTER
¼" = 1'-0"   MARCH 15, 1988
FOR: JOE RUSSO
OUTBOARD PROFILE
60' × 59½' × 20' × 4'
JAY R. BENFORD
P.O. BOX 447
ST. MICHAELS, MD 21663
(301) 745-3235

ENCLOSED LIVING SPACES:

FOC'SLE	110	SQ. FT.
ENG. RM	109	
SALOON/GALLEY	246	
MID. STRM. + HEAD	124	
MASTER STRM. + HEAD	317	
PILOTHOUSE	103	
TOTAL	1009	SQ. FT.

UPPER CABIN LAYOUT

LOWER CABIN LAYOUT

254-15

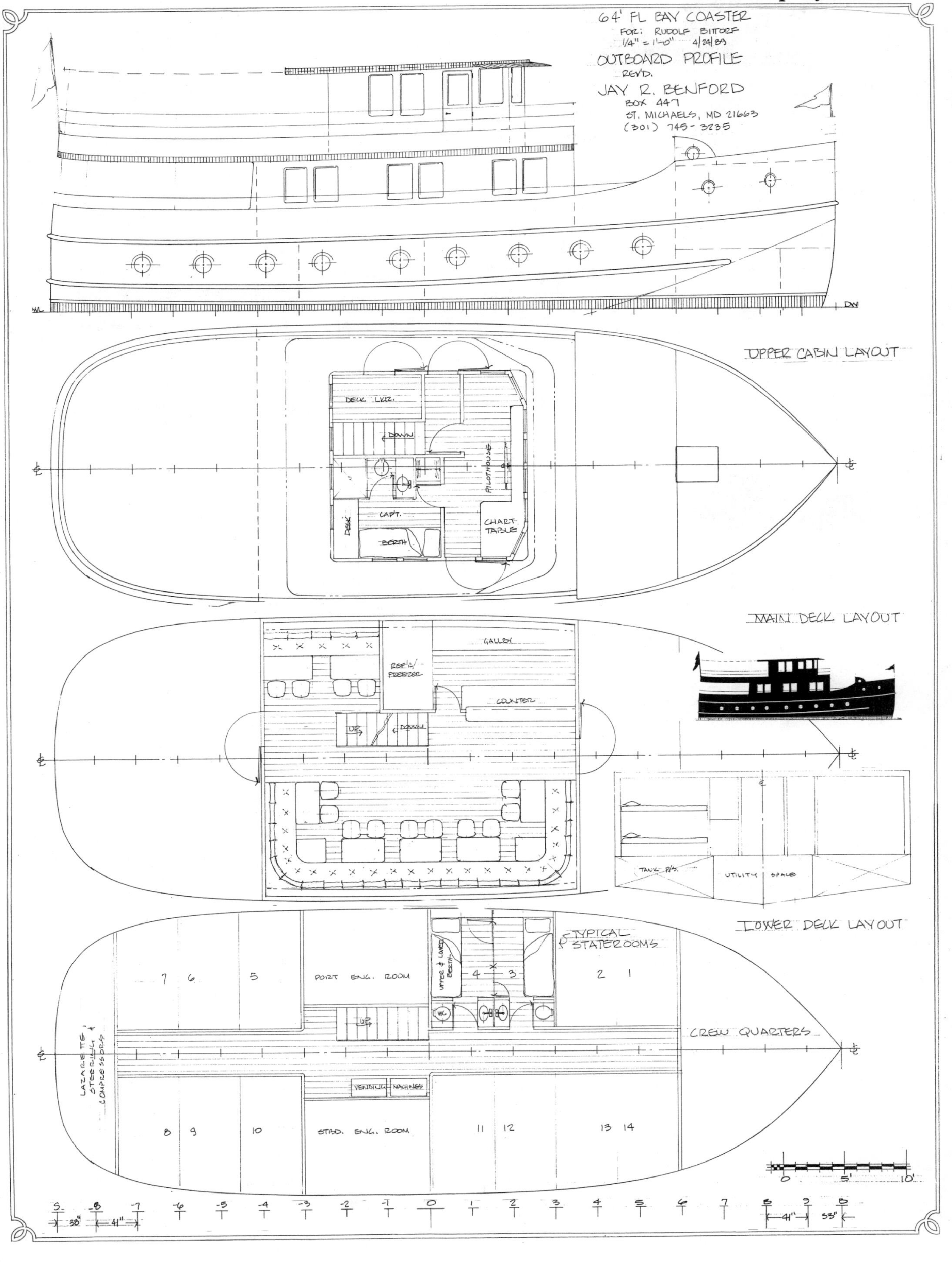

64' FL BAY COASTER
FOR: RUDOLF BITTOLF
1/4" = 1'-0"   4/24/89

OUTBOARD PROFILE
REV'D.

JAY R. BENFORD
BOX 447
ST. MICHAELS, MD 21663
(301) 745-3235

UPPER CABIN LAYOUT

DECK LKR.

DOWN

PILOTHOUSE

DESK

CAPT.

BERTH

CHART TABLE

MAIN DECK LAYOUT

GALLEY

REF & FREEZER

COUNTER

UP

DOWN

LOWER DECK LAYOUT

TANK P/S

UTILITY SPACE

TYPICAL STATEROOMS

7 6   5   PORT ENG. ROOM

UPPER & LOWER BERTH

4   3

2   1

WC

UP

CREW QUARTERS

LAZARETTE: STEERING & COUPLESS DRAG

VENTING NACHINES

8   9   10   STBD. ENG. ROOM

11 12

13 14

0   5'   10'

5 8 -7 -6 -5 -4 -3 -2 -1 0 1 2 3 4 5 6 7

30" 41"

41" 53"

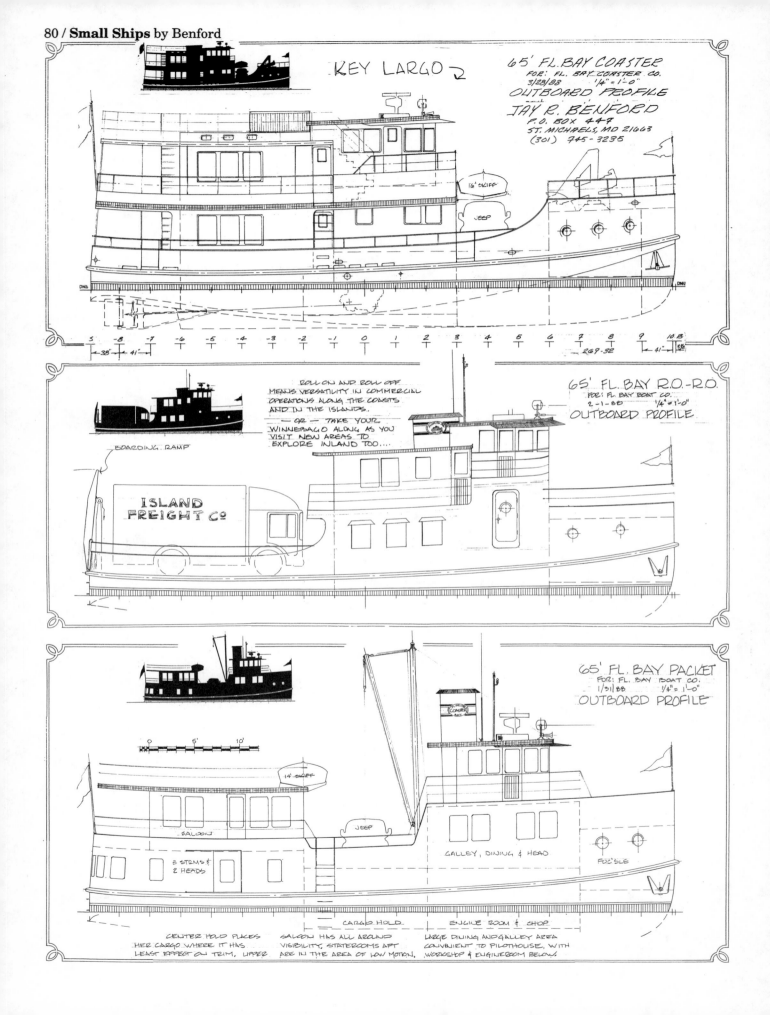

KEY LARGO

65' FL. BAY COASTER
FOR: FL. BAY COASTER CO.
3/28/88   1/4" = 1'-0"
OUTBOARD PROFILE
and
JAY R. BENFORD
P.O. BOX 447
ST. MICHAELS, MD 21663
(301) 745-3235

16' SKIFF

JEEP

DWL   DWL

5 -8 -7 -6 -5 -4 -3 -2 -1 0 1 2 3 4 5 6 7 8 9 10 B
|-35'-|-41'-| 269-32 |-41'-| 5½'

ROLL ON AND ROLL OFF
MEANS VERSATILITY IN COMMERCIAL
OPERATIONS ALONG THE COASTS
AND IN THE ISLANDS.
— OR — TAKE YOUR
WINNEBAGO ALONG AS YOU
VISIT NEW AREAS TO
EXPLORE INLAND TOO....

65' FL. BAY R.O.-R.O.
FOR: FL. BAY BOAT CO.
2-1-88   1/4" = 1'-0"
OUTBOARD PROFILE

BOARDING RAMP

ISLAND
FREIGHT CO

65' FL. BAY PACKET
FOR: FL. BAY BOAT CO.
1/31/88   1/4" = 1'-0"
OUTBOARD PROFILE

0   5'   10'

14' SKIFF

SALOON

JEEP

2 STRMS &
2 HEADS

GALLEY, DINING & HEAD

FOC'SLE

CARGO HOLD   ENGINE ROOM & SHOP

CENTER HOLD PLACES   SALOON HAS ALL AROUND   LARGE DINING AND GALLEY AREA
HER CARGO WHERE IT HAS   VISIBILITY, STATEROOMS AFT   CONVENIENT TO PILOTHOUSE, WITH
LEAST EFFECT ON TRIM. UPPER ARE IN THE AREA OF LOW MOTION.   WORKSHOP & ENGINEROOM BELOW.

NOTES:

1. FUEL TANKS; TO BE FULL DEPTH OF HULL, BOTTOM TO MAIN DECK, & SPACED OFF ₵ AS NOTED.

2. HOLDING TANK: ALSO FULL DEPTH OF HULL FROM BOTTOM ₵ TO MAIN DECK, LOCATED AS DIMENSIONED.

ENCLOSED LIVING SPACES:

ENG. RM + BASEMENT	212 FT²
HOLD	123
MID STRM + HEAD	185
SALOON & GALLEY	292
FOC'SLE	135
PILOTHOUSE	119
MASTER STRM + HEAD	239
TOTAL	1305 SQ.FT.

KEY LARGO

65' FL. BAY COASTER
1/4" = 1'-0"   4-5-88
FOR: FL BAY COASTER CO.

DECK PLAN
REVISED · 3/29/88 / 4-14-88 / 6-21-88

JAY R. BENFORD 8-11-88
P. O. BOX 447
ST. MICHAELS, MD 21663
(301) 745-3235

SKYLIGHT   30"x65"x28" OPTIONAL HOT TUB   CARGO HATCHES   CRANE BASE   15x23 HATCH   SCUTTLE

← SEE SHEET 100 FOR MORE DETAILS →   ← SEE SHEET 64 FOR MORE DETAILS →

UPPER CABIN LAYOUT

DOWN   DRESSER   KING SIZE BERTH   30"x60" SHOWER   WC   HANGING LKR.   BOOKCASE   UP PASS

LOWER CABIN ARR'GT

SHOWER HEAD & HOSE BIB   BOARDING GATE   DOWN   UP   STERN PLATFORM   REF/FREEZER   RANGE   TUB/SHOWER   HNG. LKR.   SHELF-TOP AT 5' ABOVE SOLE   DOWN TO ENG. RM.   WET LKR.   BUREAU   HNG. LKR.   DESK   JEEP WRANGLER 4x4   BOARDING GATE P/S.   E.R. VENT DUCT P/S.   LAV/SHOWER   WC.   BERTH   DRESSER   CHAIN LKR.   BERTH   HNG. LKR.   ICE MAKER

← SEE SHEET 103 FOR ARR'T DETAILS →

HULL ARRANGEMENT

675 GALS FUEL   700 GSL WATER   CAT 3208T 375 HP DSL   700 GALS FUEL   SHELVES   SHELVES   DRYER/ WASHER   EXTENDS DOWN TO 2 BLG LEVEL   BOW THRUSTER   WORK BENCH   WT   CARGO HOLD   WT   COLLISION B'HD   500 GALS HOLDING   FREEZER CHEST AHUG OVER   SHELVES   675 GALS FUEL   700 GAL WATER   BERRY CON   670 GALS FUEL   SHELVES

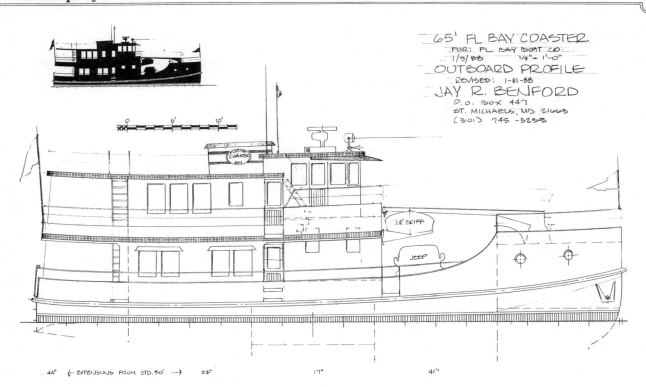

65' FL BAY COASTER
FOR: FL BAY BOAT CO
7/9/88   1/4" = 1'-0"
OUTBOARD PROFILE
REVISED: 1-31-88
JAY R. BENFORD
P.O. BOX 447
ST. MICHAELS, MD 21663
(301) 745-3233

14' SKIFF

JEEP

44" ← EXTENSIONS FROM STD. 50' → 24"   17"   41"

STRETCHED TO 65' THE COASTER
COMES INTO HER OWN. ALL THE
FEATURES OF THE 50 ARE EXPANDED
OUT, CREATING MORE ROOM, MORE
STORAGE, MORE SEA-KEEPING
ABILITY, & A UNIQUE, HANDSOME
APPEARANCE.

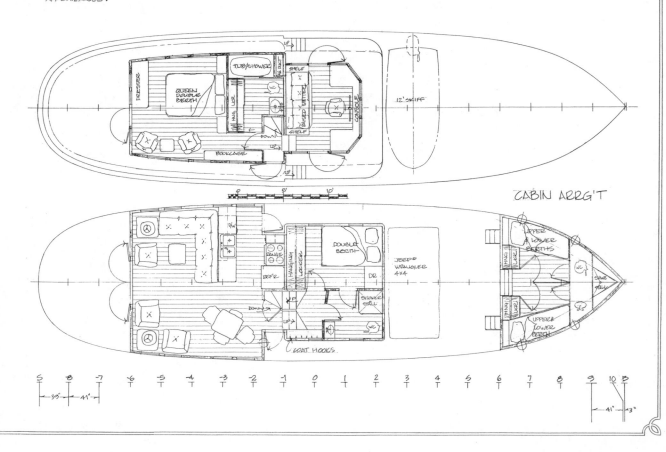

CABIN ARRG'T

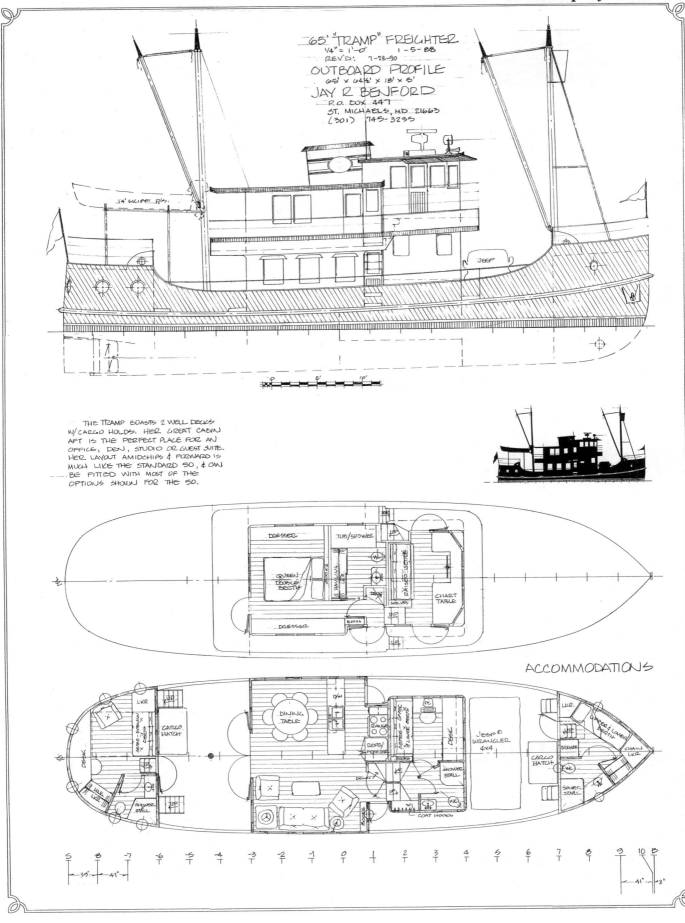

65' "TRAMP" FREIGHTER
1/4" = 1'-0"   1-5-88
REV'D: 7-28-90
OUTBOARD PROFILE
65' x 64½' x 18' x 5'
JAY R BENFORD
P.O. BOX 447
ST. MICHAELS, MD 21663
(301) 745-3235

THE TRAMP BOASTS 2 WELL DECKS
W/ CARGO HOLDS. HER GREAT CABIN
AFT IS THE PERFECT PLACE FOR AN
OFFICE, DEN, STUDIO OR GUEST SUITE.
HER LAYOUT AMIDSHIPS & FORWARD IS
MUCH LIKE THE STANDARD 50, & CAN
BE FITTED WITH MOST OF THE
OPTIONS SHOWN FOR THE 50.

ACCOMMODATIONS

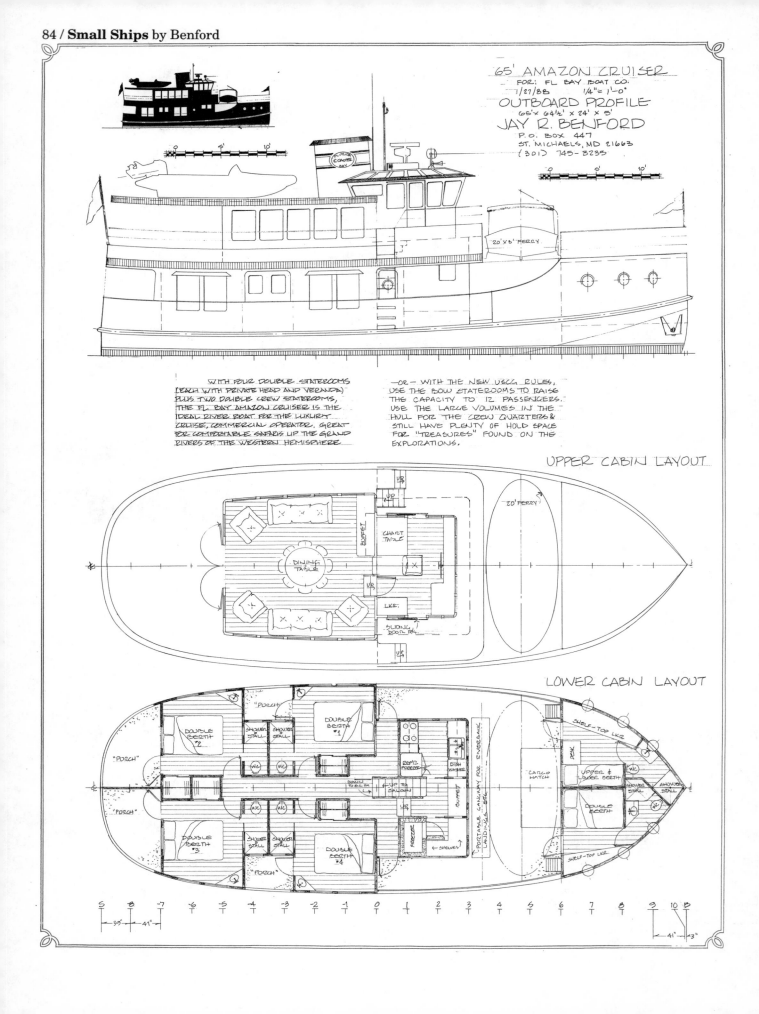

65' AMAZON CRUISER
FOR: FL BAY BOAT CO.
7/27/88   1/4" = 1'-0"
OUTBOARD PROFILE
65' x 64½' x 24' x 5'
JAY R. BENFORD
P.O. BOX 447
ST. MICHAELS, MD 21663
(301) 745-3235

20' x 8' FERRY

WITH FOUR DOUBLE STATEROOMS (EACH WITH PRIVATE HEAD AND VERANDA) PLUS TWO DOUBLE CREW STATEROOMS, THE FL BAY AMAZON CRUISER IS THE IDEAL RIVER BOAT FOR THE LUXURY CRUISE, COMMERCIAL OPERATOR. GREAT FOR COMFORTABLE SAFARIS UP THE GRAND RIVERS OF THE WESTERN HEMISPHERE

— OR — WITH THE NEW USCG RULES, USE THE BOW STATEROOMS TO RAISE THE CAPACITY TO 12 PASSENGERS. USE THE LARGE VOLUMES IN THE HULL FOR THE CREW QUARTERS & STILL HAVE PLENTY OF HOLD SPACE FOR "TREASURES" FOUND ON THE EXPLORATIONS.

UPPER CABIN LAYOUT

20' FERRY
BUFFET
CHART TABLE
DINING TABLE
LKR.
SLIDING DOOR R4.

LOWER CABIN LAYOUT

DOUBLE BERTH #2
"PORCH"
SHOWER STALL
SHOWER STALL
DOUBLE BERTH #1
REF'R. FREEZER
DISH WASHER
SHELF-TOP LKR
DECK
CARGO HATCH
UPPER & LOWER BERTH
WC
WC
DOWN TO ENG RM
UP TO SALOON
BUFFET
PORTABLE GANGWAY FOR RIVERBANK LANDINGS ETC.
DOUBLE BERTH
SHOWER STALL
SHOWER STALL
"PORCH"
DOUBLE BERTH #3
SHOWER STALL
SHOWER STALL
DOUBLE BERTH #4
FREEZER
SHOWER
"PORCH"
SHELF-TOP LKR

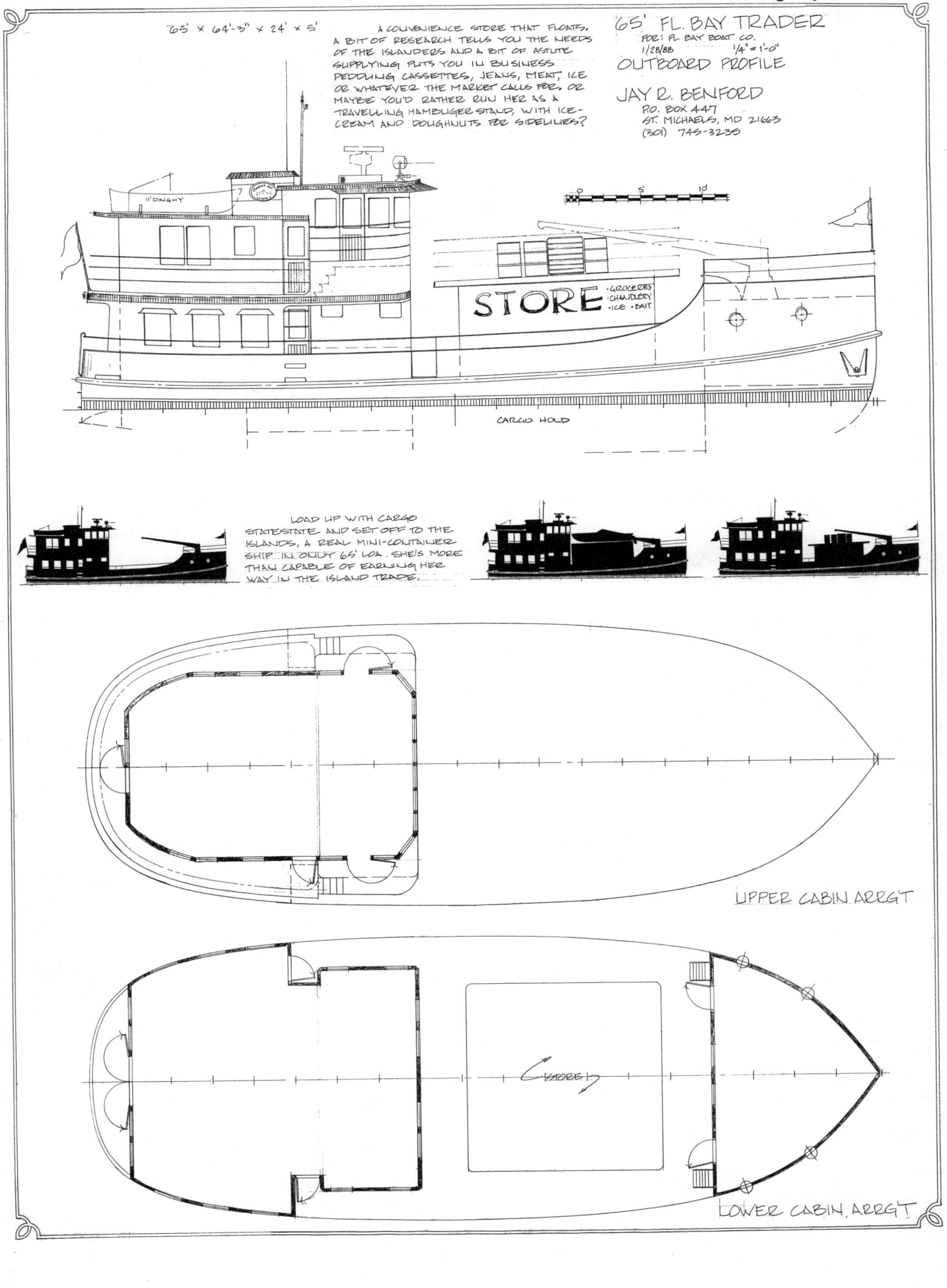

'65' X 64'-3" X 24' X 5'

A CONVENIENCE STORE THAT FLOATS.
A BIT OF RESEARCH TELLS YOU THE NEEDS
OF THE ISLANDERS AND A BIT OF ASTUTE
SUPPLYING PUTS YOU IN BUSINESS
PEDDLING CASSETTES, JEANS, MEAT, ICE
OR WHATEVER THE MARKET CALLS FOR. OR
MAYBE YOU'D RATHER RUN HER AS A
TRAVELLING HAMBURGER STAND, WITH ICE-
CREAM AND DOUGHNUTS FOR SIDELINES?

65' FL. BAY TRADER
FOR: FL. BAY BOAT CO.
1/28/88   1/4" = 1'-0"
OUTBOARD PROFILE

JAY R. BENFORD
P.O. BOX 447
ST. MICHAELS, MD 21663
(301) 745-3235

11' DINGHY

STORE
· GROCERIES
· CHANDLERY
· ICE · BAIT

CARGO HOLD

LOAD UP WITH CARGO
STATESIDE AND SET OFF TO THE
ISLANDS, A REAL MINI-CONTAINER
SHIP IN ONLY 65' LOA. SHE'S MORE
THAN CAPABLE OF EARNING HER
WAY IN THE ISLAND TRADE.

UPPER CABIN ARRG'T

STORE

LOWER CABIN ARRG'T

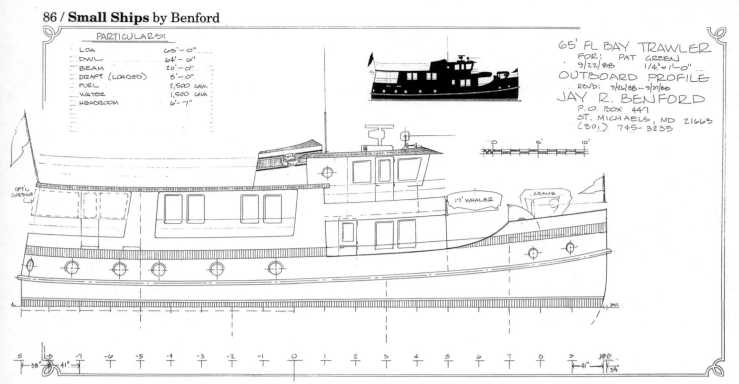

65' Trawler Yacht

This vessel is an extension of our design philosophy as exemplified in the freighters, of simplicity and rugged construction. We've applied it to the trawler yacht as we have to the variety of freighter designs in this book.

The result is a rugged little ship, with all the comforts and features usually found on trawler yachts.

We did a number of studies on the profile for the boat, and these are shown here. Some of the profile variations require moving the foc'sle accommodations aft a bit, to take into account the finer bow shape and the overhanging

stem. While reducing the size of the hold, this would let her be driven at higher speed in rough going. This is a mixed blessing, for a slower speed is usually more comfortable in rough weather.

This saloon shows two different sides, with and without side decks. I'd prefer the walkaround decks, but some services require maximizing the interior volume.

The accommodations in the hull also show a variation for the middle staterooms. They could be converted to small meeting rooms, or opened across the centerline into one good sized room, for a meeting, a larger party, or a big playroom for the kids.

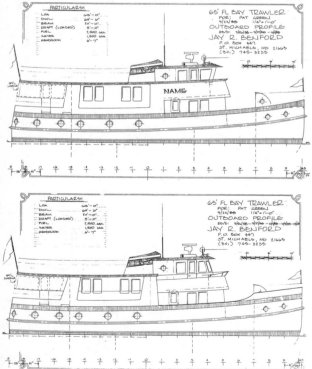

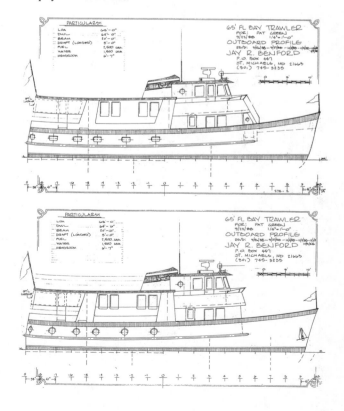

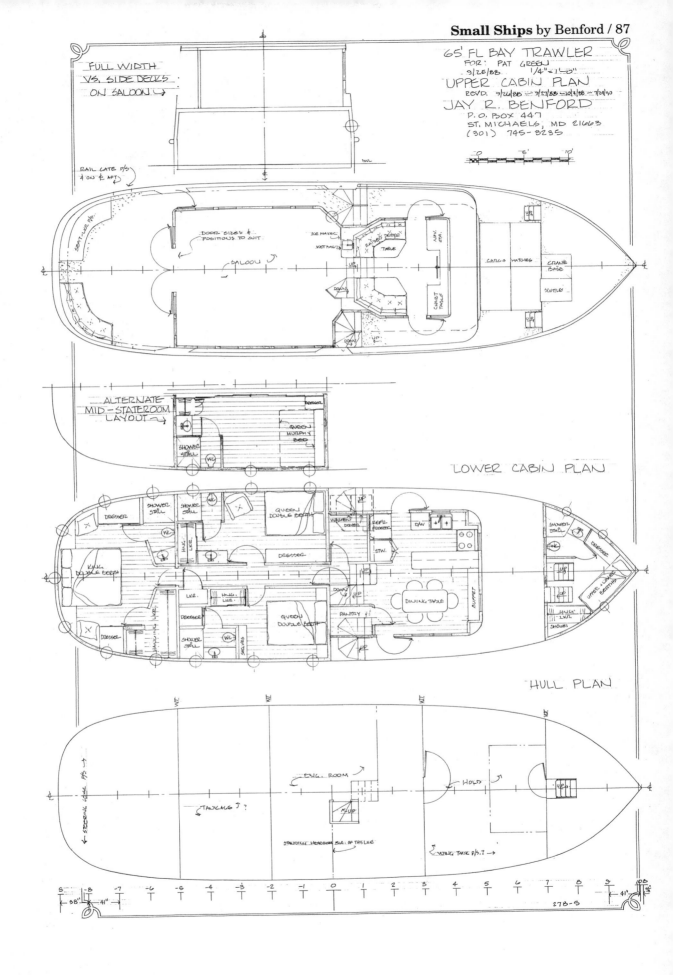

FULL WIDTH
VS. SIDE DECKS
ON SALOON

65' FL BAY TRAWLER
FOR: PAT GREEN
9/26/88   1/4"=1'-0"
UPPER CABIN PLAN
REVD. 9/26/88 - 9/27/88 - 10/3/88 - 7/24/90
JAY R. BENFORD
P.O. BOX 447
ST. MICHAELS, MD 21663
(301) 745-3235

SALOON

ALTERNATE
MID-STATEROOM
LAYOUT

LOWER CABIN PLAN

HULL PLAN

278-S

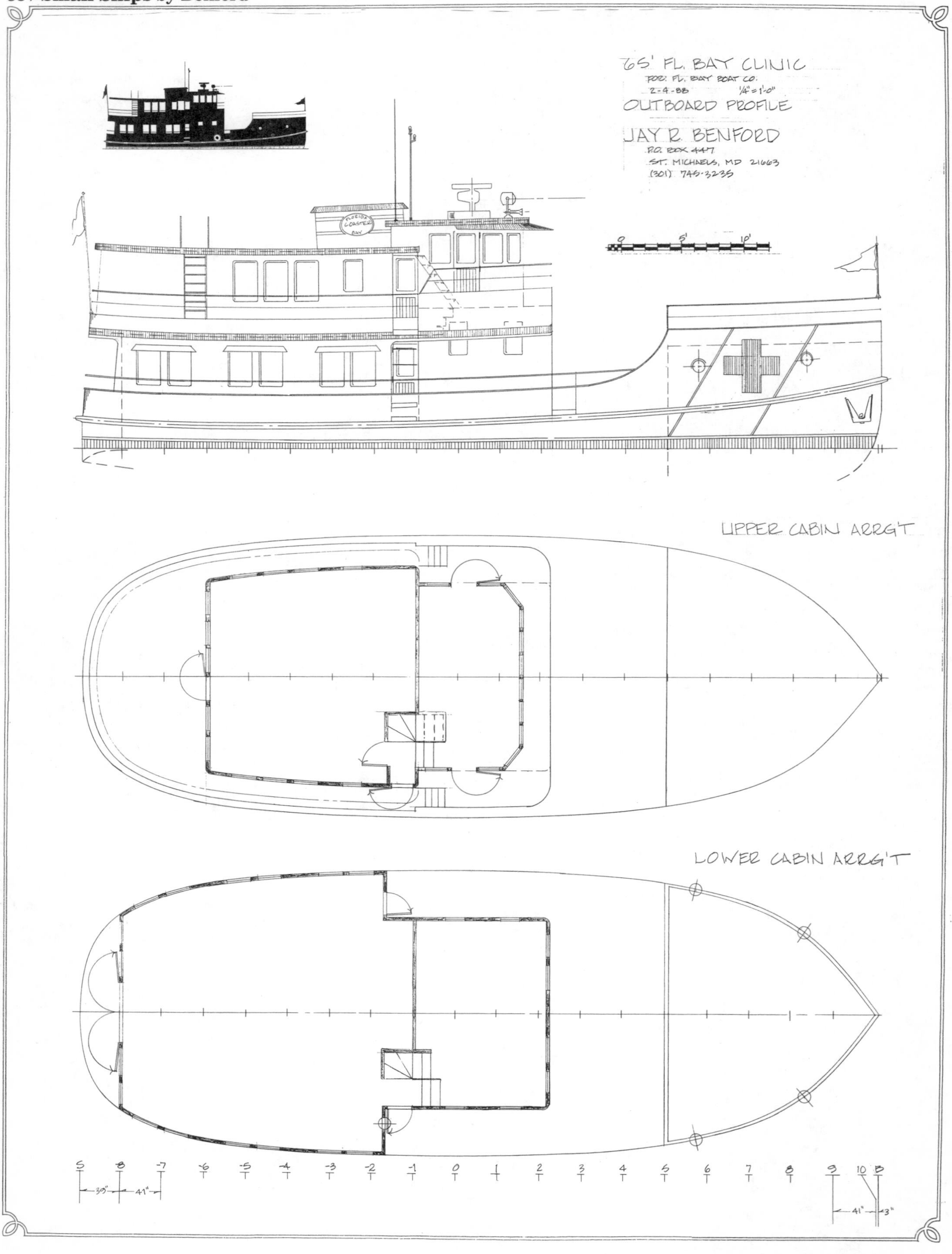

65' FL. BAY CLINIC
FOR: FL. BAY BOAT CO.
2-4-88
1/4" = 1'-0"
OUTBOARD PROFILE
JAY R. BENFORD
P.O. BOX 447
ST. MICHAELS, MD 21663
(301) 745-3235
0
5'
10'
FLORIDA COASTER BAY
UPPER CABIN ARRG'T
LOWER CABIN ARRG'T
S
-8
-7
-6
-5
-4
-3
-2
-1
0
1
2
3
4
5
6
7
8
9
10
B
39"
41"
41"
3"

Future Freighters

Will a larger freighter better suit your needs? Do you need more room for more staterooms? Would you like even roomier spaces on board? Would you like to have greater cargo capacity?

The design philosophy that has made these boats so successful can readily be extended to other sizes. The sketches shown on this page are some of the ideas we've considered for larger ones.

The U.S. Coast Guard's new regulations, when put into effect, will permit carrying 12 passengers on uninspected vessels (yachts), instead of 6 as currently allowed. This will open a world of opportunity to those who would like to run their own mini-cruiseship.

The mini-cruiseship could be run on rivers and canals where a larger vessel would not fit, and where there is lighter demand for tours. It would also make for customization of the cruises, with the charterees participating in setting the itinerary, instead of being taken along with the herd on a large ship.

How about the Seattle to Southeast Alaska route? Or a circumnavigation of southern Florida and the Everglades? The choice is yours.

Or, would you just like a larger cruising vessel. Let us know what you'd like and we'll be happy to work with you in creating your new small ship.

80' TRAMP

85' FREIGHTER

WHY NOT?
YOU'VE GOT THE TOYS AND THE TIME TO ENJOY THEM, THE 100-FOOTER HAS THE ROOM TO CARRY THEM AND YOU ON HIGH ADVENTURE WHETHER DOWN THE COAST OR UP THE RIVERS OR ACROSS THE SEAS.

100' FL. BAY COASTER
1/8" = 1'-0"   1/30/88
FOR: FL. BAY BOAT CO.
OUTBOARD PROFILE

JAY R. BENFORD
P. O. BOX 447
ST. MICHAELS, MD 21663
(301) 745-3235

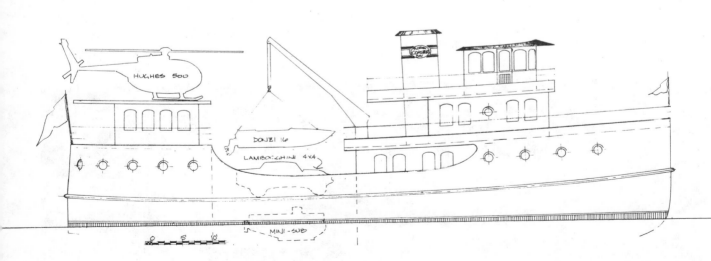

HUGHES 500

DONZI 16

LAMBORGHINI 4X4

MINI-SUB

Part 4 — Ferries & Excursion Boats

20' Ferry

Paul Miller has now built three fleets of the 20' ferries, which are running in Victoria and Vancouver, British Columbia. They have proven successful workhorses, carrying their passengers through all sorts of conditions, and carrying tremendous numbers of them. The two Vancouver fleets did heroic duty during Expo '86 there, and were a big hit with the passengers.

The Canadian versions have been operated with a normal load of 12 passengers. USCG licensed versions for water-front touring and harbor hopping can have capacities of 18 passengers. Additional uses could be for Yacht Club shuttle service or service to a private island.

Having very low operating costs in addition to low construction costs, they are a great success.

The Friday Harbor Ferry version has cruising accommodations for a couple. We've lowered the cabin sole to get standing headroom, put in a good galley, and provided for an enclosed head with a shower. She has all the comforts of a small motorhome, without the worry about finding a paved road to the places you want to visit. It's also easier to get off the beaten path and find a place with some privacy.

24' Ferry

The 24' Ferry was designed as an expansion of the 20-footer, with the idea being to double the carrying capacity of the ferry, yet be able to operate with the same, single crew member.

The extra size over the 20-footer gives better standing headroom and more room for the passengers to stretch their legs when seated.

Her power requirements are a bit higher, but the actual installed power will likely be the same, since the 20-footers ended up overpowered in the desire to get smoother 2-cylinder engines in them. Thus, fuel consumption will be a bit higher, but probably a bit less on a per passenger basis.

The 24' Friday Harbor Ferry version has all the comfortable features found on land-based motorhomes. And, unlike motorhomes, you can get off the beaten path more easily and find places with privacy to spend the night.

There are two separate sleeping areas, in the pilothouse and the convertible dinette. The roomy head has a separate tub and shower space. The galley has a refrigerator, sink, stove and storage spaces. The desk makes a nice work space for a PC, a typewriter, or doing chart work.

The pilothouse is well lit and provides a commanding view for the helmsman. The raised double bed will make a good seat for daytime operations. The opening to the lower cabin can be closed off to give a private stateroom at night.

26' North Channel Ferry

Evolved from the 24' Ferry, the 26' North Channel Ferry has a similar layout, with slightly more room due to the extra beam and length. The hull form was modified to have a more conventional bow shape to take the steeper seas expected in cruising the North Channel and going South for the winter.

She'd make a great liveaboard for a young couple or a summer home for a small family.

Paul Miller's shop with two of the Vancouver Aquabus fleet under construction, along with two of our Cape Scott 36' double ended cutters, and one of the first of the Victoria Harbor Ferries in service. Photos courtesy of the builder.

JAY R. BENFORD
P.O. BOX 447 ~ ST. MICHAELS, MD 21663

SPIRIT of FALSE CREEK

6 to 10 HP DIESEL

24"   24"

20' FALSE CREEK FERRY

SEAT

PILOT SEAT   HELM   INSTRUMENTS

SEAT

8" MOORING CLEATS

6-10 HP DIESEL

24"   24"

20' FRIDAY HARBOR FERRY

SHELVES   STEP

RANGE

HEAD

SHOWER GRATE

SLIDING DOOR

SHELF TOP LKR.   DRAWERS

COUNTER

REFR. UNDER   PILOT SEAT   WHEEL   INSTRUMENTS

DINING TABLE LOWERS TO MAKE DOUBLE BERTH

STEP

8" MOORING CLEATS

SLIDING DOOR P/S.

PARTICULARS:	
LOA	20'-0"
DWL	19'-0"
BEAM	8'-0"
DRAFT	2'-0"
FREEBOARD:	
FWD. & AFT	2'-4½"
LEAST	1'-2½"
DISPL. (CRUISING TRIM)	4,260 LBS.
DISPL./L. RATIO	277
PRISMATIC COEF.	.605
LBS./IN. IMMERSION	580
FUEL	20 GALS.
WATER	50 GALS.
HEADROOM	6'-1"

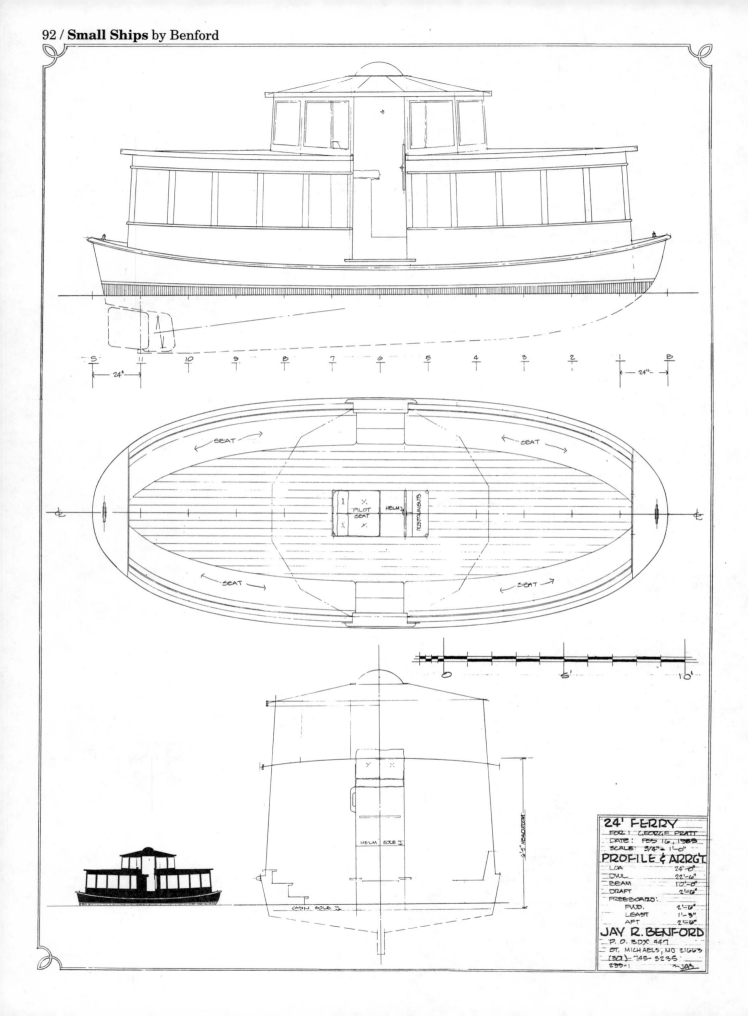

SEAT

SEAT

PILOT
SEAT

HELM

SEAT

SEAT

HELM SOLE J

CABIN SOLE J

24" FERRY
FOR: GEORGE PRATT
DATE: FEB 16, 1989
SCALE: 3/4"=1'-0"
PROFILE & ARRG'T.
LOA   24'-0"
DWL   22'-6"
BEAM   10'-0"
DRAFT   2'-0"
FREEBOARD:
  FWD.   2'-0"
  LEAST   1'-3"
  AFT   2'-0"
JAY R. BENFORD
P. O. BOX 447
ST. MICHAELS, MD 21663
(301) 745-3235
233-1

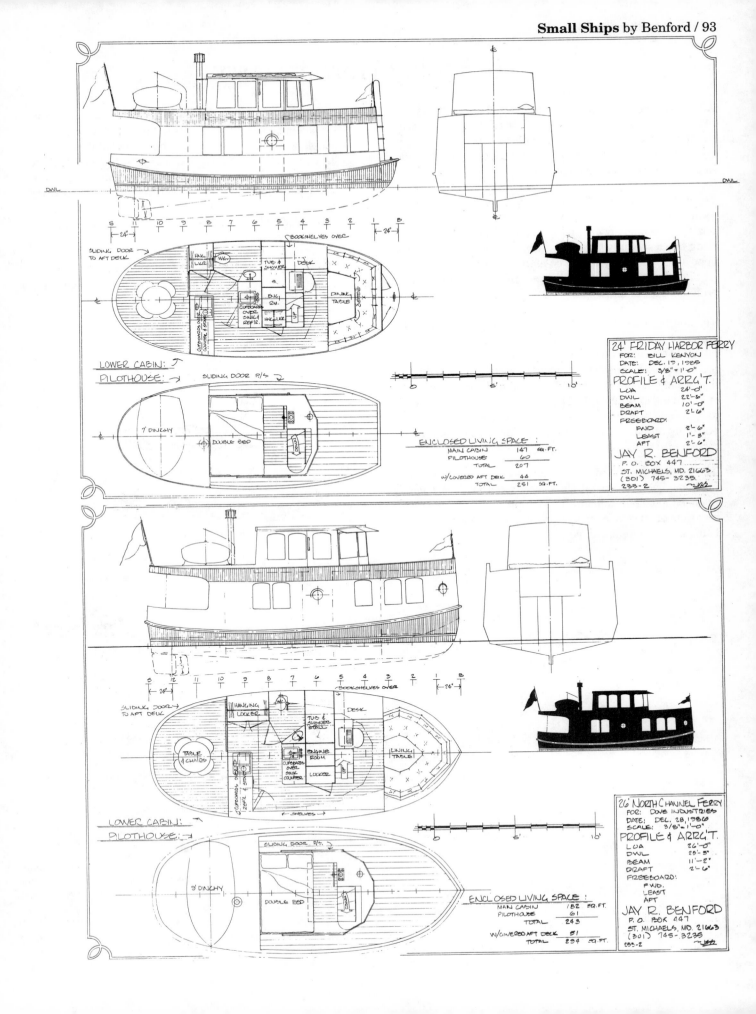

DWL

BOOKSHELVES OVER

SLIDING DOOR TO AFT DECK

HANG. LKR.

TUB & SHOWER

DESK

BNG. RM.

DINING TABLE

CUPBOARDS OVER SINK & REFR.

HANG. LKR.

LOWER CABIN:

PILOTHOUSE:

SLIDING DOOR P/S

7' DINGHY

(4) DOUBLE BED

STOVE

ENCLOSED LIVING SPACE:

MAIN CABIN .... 147 SQ. FT.
PILOTHOUSE 60
TOTAL 207

W/ COVERED AFT DECK 44
TOTAL 251 SQ. FT.

24' FRIDAY HARBOR FERRY
FOR: BILL KENYON
DATE: DEC. 15, 1988
SCALE: 3/8" = 1'-0"
PROFILE & ARR'G'T.
LOA 24'-0"
DWL 22'-6"
BEAM 10'-0"
DRAFT 2'-6"
FREEBOARD:
FWD 2'-6"
LEAST 1'-3"
AFT 2'-6"
JAY R. BENFORD
P.O. BOX 447
ST. MICHAELS, MD. 21663
(301) 745-3235
233-2

BOOKSHELVES OVER

SLIDING DOOR TO AFT DECK

HANGING LOCKER

WC.

TUB & SHOWER STALL

DESK

TABLE & CHAIRS

ENGINE ROOM

DINING TABLE

CUPBOARDS OVER SINK COUNTER

LOCKER

SHELVES

LOWER CABIN:

PILOTHOUSE:

SLIDING DOOR P/S

9' DINGHY

DOUBLE BED

STOVE

ENCLOSED LIVING SPACE:
MAIN CABIN .... 182 SQ. FT.
PILOTHOUSE 61
TOTAL 243

W/ COVERED AFT DECK 51
TOTAL 294 SQ. FT.

26' NORTH CHANNEL FERRY
FOR: DOVE INDUSTRIES
DATE: DEC. 28, 1988
SCALE: 3/8" = 1'-0"
PROFILE & ARR'G'T.
LOA 26'-0"
DWL 25'-5"
BEAM 11'-2"
DRAFT 2'-6"
FREEBOARD:
FWD.
LEAST
AFT
JAY R. BENFORD
P.O. BOX 447
ST. MICHAELS, MD. 21663
(301) 745-3235
233-2

30' Friday Harbor Ferry

Almost two decades ago I decided that a small boat styled like a ferry boat would have the most useful room in it as a liveaboard boat. It's tremendous volume would permit houselike spaces and get away from the feeling of camping in tight quarters found on many boats.

The styling of the boat like a working ferry would also get away from the stigma usually associated with "houseboats." Too many people think of a houseboat as something like a shoddily built house trailer on a boxy hull. The appearance of a ferry would be more socially acceptable, particularly for someone leaving a sailboat for something with more room in it.

The ability to pull waterskiers at speed, while consuming a gallon or two of fuel per mile does not fit in well with a boat that will have all of one's worldly possessions aboard, for weight is the biggest detriment to speed. Weight does help steady the motion of the boat, and make her more comfortable to be aboard. Thus, we've designed the ferry to be an easily driven displacement hull, keeping her powering requirements modest. She has good capability to carry a load gracefully.

The original version of this design was called the Waterbed 30, named after the bed in the master stateroom. She was intended to be a liveaboard for a couple, with all the comforts of an efficiency apartment, plus the mobility of being able to unplug and go cruising.

Her design was published in a number of magazines, and we had unprecedented response. She struck a chord in people who wanted to live on a boat, but didn't want to have to compromise away the comforts they knew ashore. The later version, for which construction plans are available (for building in plywood and epoxy), is the 30' Ferry Yacht. We've swapped the master stateroom into the pilothouse and created a home office or den in the forward, lower cabin.

The section through the pilothouse shows the bank of drawers for chart storage, allowing for literally hundreds of charts to be stored flat and not folded.

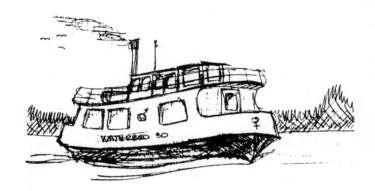

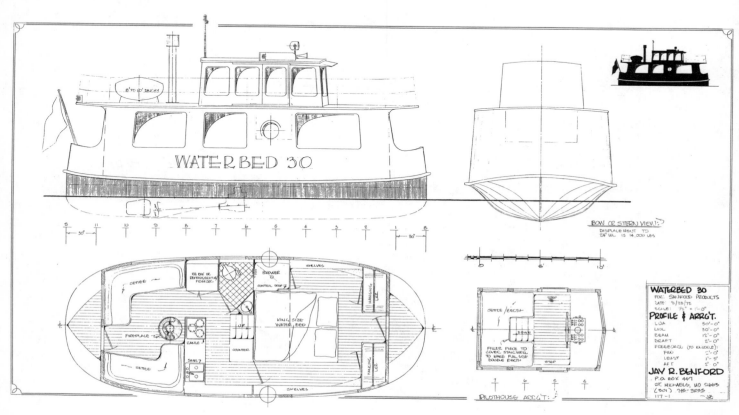

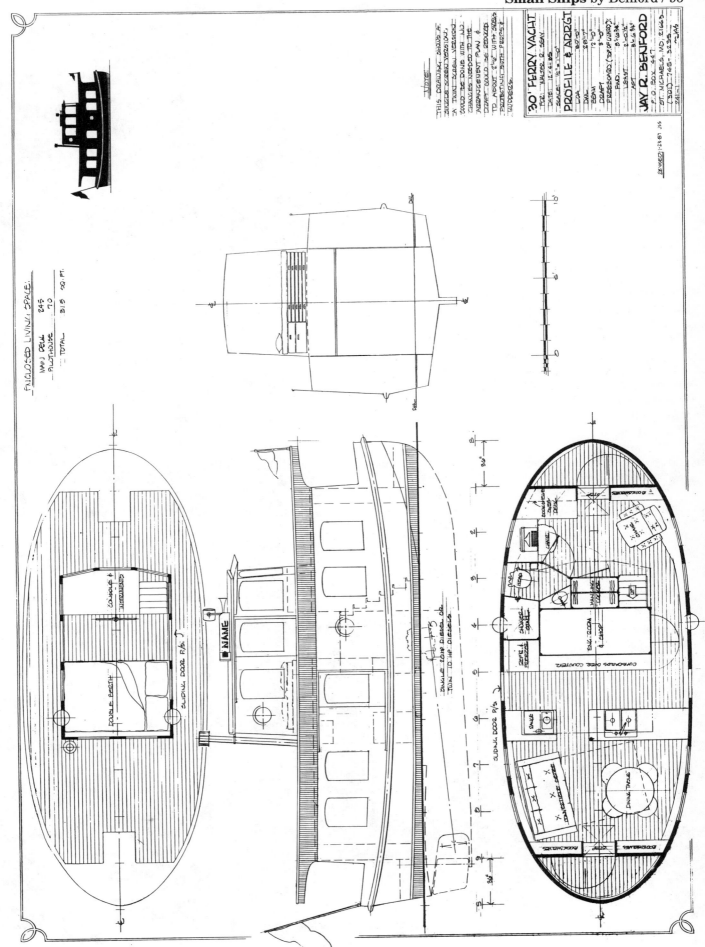

ENCLOSED LIVING SPACE:
MAIN DECK   245
PILOTHOUSE   70
   = TOTAL   315 SQ. FT.

NOTE:

THIS DRAWING SHOWS A SINGLE SCREW VERSION. A TWIN SCREW VERSION COULD BE DONE WITH NO CHANGES NEEDED TO THE ARRANGEMENT PLAN & DRAFT COULD BE REDUCED TO ABOUT 2'6" WITH SKEGS PROTECTING BOTH PROPS & RUDDERS.

'30' FERRY YACHT
FOR: WALTER R. SEAY
DATE: 12-11-85
SCALE: 1/4"=1'-0"

LOA   30'-0"
LWL   28'-0"
BEAM   12'-0"
DRAFT   3'-0"
FREEBOARD (TOP OF GUARD):
  FWD.   3'10½"
  LEAST   2'1-0½"
  AFT   2'6¾"

JAY R. BENFORD
P.O. BOX 447
ST. MICHAELS, MD. 21663
(301) 745- 3235
241-1   JRM

REVISED 1-23-61 JSS

PROFILE & ARR'GT.

SINGLE 20HP DIESEL OR TWIN 10 HP DIESELS

SLIDING DOOR P/S

NAME

DOUBLE BERTH
CONSOLE &
INSTRUMENTS

DANGEROUS LOCKER
DINING TABLE
DROPLEAVES
STOWAGE
GALLEY
REFRIG. & FREEZER
HANGING LOCKER
SHOWER SPACE
HEAD
W.C.
DOUBLE DECK
SLIDING DOOR P/S
BED-ROOM & SHOP
CUPBOARDS OVER COUNTER

34' Friday Harbor Ferry

This design was the result of a request for a roomier version of the 30-footer, for more comfortable living aboard. The increase in size from 30 to 34' in length and from 12 to 14' of beam make a great difference in spaciousness.

The head has room for a bathtub with shower and there is a washer and dryer stackset too. A house-size side-by-side refrigerator and freezer can be run off shore power, a small generator, or an inverter.

The version with the beach umbrella on the aft deck shows another usage for these versatile boats. This is a concept for floating hotel rooms, with two independent rooms. They share a common entry and galley on the lower level. Each unit has its own private head with shower stall and its own private aft deck.

We could have made a version that was to be lightly outfitted and driven at high speed. However, we felt that the operating philosophy should be that once you were aboard, you were already where you really wanted to be. Moving the boat might be for a change of scenery, although cruising in one would be fun too.

Look over the following designs and imagine how it would be to live on one yourself. We've little ones and big ones. Some with open "porches" forward and some with more conventional enclosed bows. Some laid out as liveaboards, some as offices, and some as passenger or excursion boats.

The first of the 34' ferries was built by professional builder Garry Parenteau and is home for his family. These photos show the rooms saloon, galley and forward staterooms, and her afloat being completed.

Choice Waterfront Homes

Available with panoramic marine views from Puget Sound to Alaska or Florida to Maine. An ideal liveaboard or retirement home or vacation home, the 34' Friday Harbor Ferry offers a majestic variety of unique marine park settings, each available without ever leaving home. These luxury homes offer low maintenance fiberglass and teak exterior and warm wood interior with all utilities installed, including washer, dryer, bathtub and fireplace. Two bedrooms, complete kitchen, large sundeck, and two viewing porches. Economical diesel power and large tanks provide for safe and low-cost operation. Neighbors too noisy? Move your house. Tired of mowing the lawn and raking leaves? Try ferry boat living for fast relief.

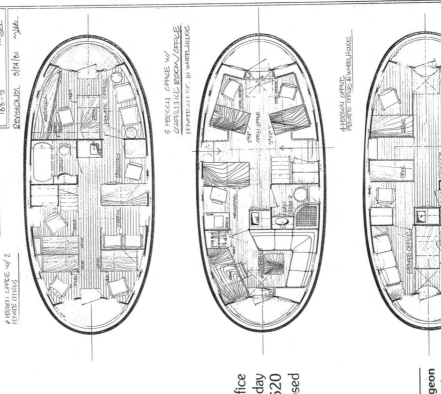

FRIDAY HARBOR FERRY

From: JAY R. BENFORD
Date: DEC. 16, 1979
Scale: 1/4" = 1'-0"

OFFICE VERSION

LOA	34'-0"
LWL	34'-0"
BEAM	14'-0"
DRAFT	2'-3"
FREEBOARD: (TOP OF GUARD)	
FWD	2'-6"
LEAST	1'-6"
AFT	2'-6"

JAY R. BENFORD
P.O. BOX 447
ST. MICHAELS, MD 21663
(301) 745-3235
183-3

REVISIONS: 3/24/81

Shown here is the office version of the Friday Harbor Ferry. It has 520 square feet of enclosed living space.

NOTES:

① INTERIOR LIVING SPACES:
LOWER HOUSE 320 SQ. FT.
UPPER HOUSE 170
PILOTHOUSE   30
TOTAL   520 SQ. FT.

Caution: The Sturgeon Genial warns that Friday Harbor living may be addictive and habit forming.

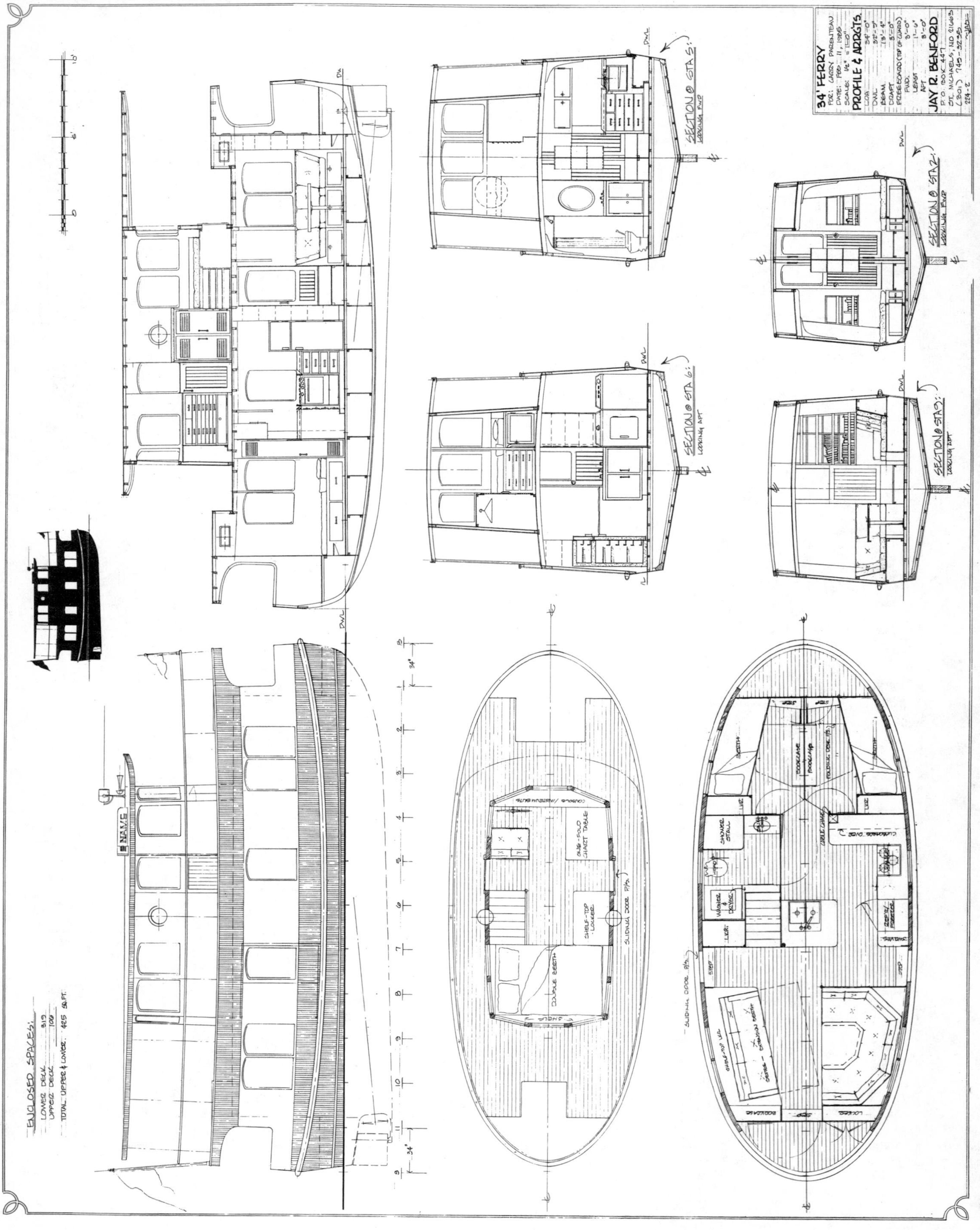
34' FERRY
FOR: GARRY PARENTEAU
DATE: FEB 11, 1985
SCALE: 1/2" = 1'-0"
PROFILE & ARRG'TS.
LOA 34'-0"
DWL 32'-7"
BEAM 13'-4"
DRAFT 3'-0"
FREEBOARD (TOP OF GUARD)
FWD. 3'-0"
LEAST 1'-6"
AFT 3'-0"
JAY R. BENFORD
P.O. BOX 447
ST. MICHAELS, MD 21663
(301) 745-3235
SECTION @ STA 5: LOOKING FWD
SECTION @ STA 2: LOOKING FWD
SECTION @ STA 6: LOOKING AFT
SECTION @ STA 9: LOOKING AFT
ENCLOSED SPACES:
LOWER DECK 319
UPPER DECK 106
TOTAL UPPER & LOWER 425 SQ.FT.
DWL

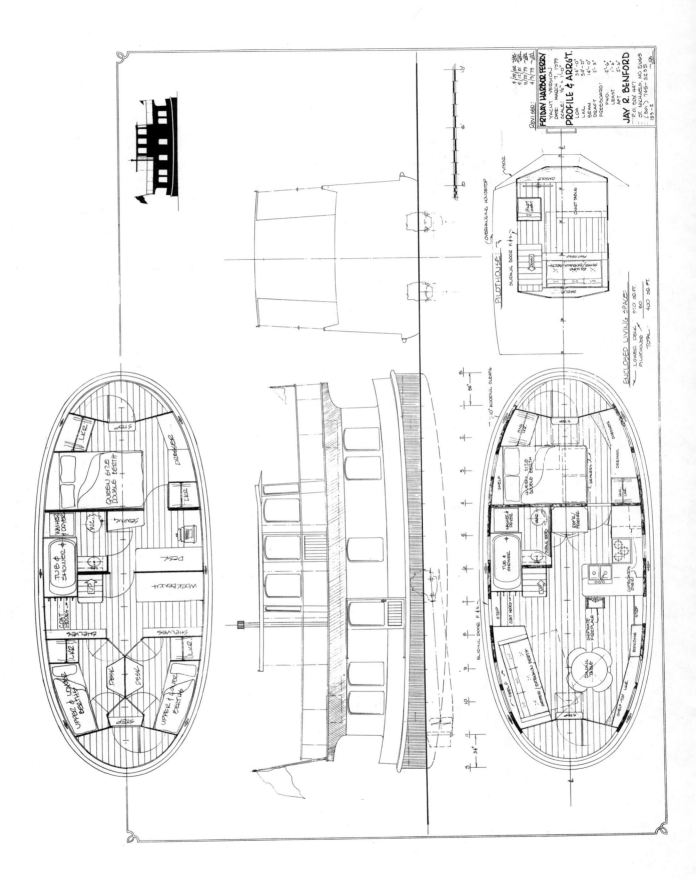

FRIDAY HARBOR FERRY
YACHT VERSION
DATE: MARCH 7, 1979
SCALE: ¼" = 1'-0"

PROFILE & ARR'G'T.

LOA	54'-0"
LWL	54'-0"
BEAM	14'-0"
DRAFT	2'-5"
FREEBOARD:	
FWD	2'-0"
LEAST	1'-0"
AFT	2'-0"

JAY R. BENFORD
P.O. BOX 447
ST. MICHAELS, MD 21663
(301) 745-5235

PILOTHOUSE

ENCLOSED LIVING SPACE:
LOWER DECK   260 SQ.FT.
PILOTHOUSE   140 SQ.FT.
TOTAL   400 SQ.FT.

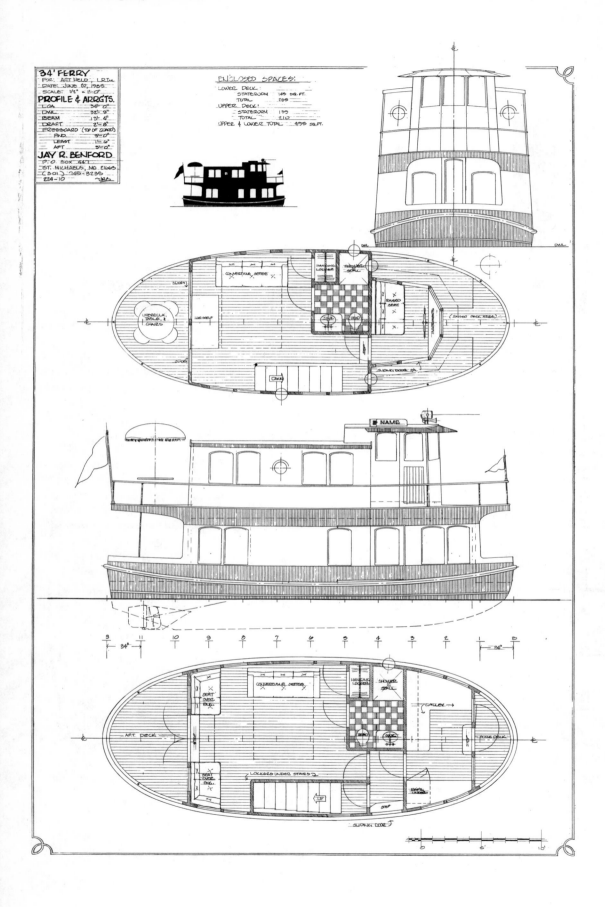

45' Friday Harbor Ferry

As spacious as a shoreside two or three bedroom home, the 45' Friday Harbor Ferry is a luxury home afloat. The 16' beam version was done originally with he idea of cold-molding or fiberglass construction. The 18' beam version was done later on, and the plans completed for building in plywood with epoxy gluing and sealing.

Her intended power is a pair of 50 to 60 horsepower diesels, with over 3:1 reduction, so they will swing good sized props. This will give reasonable fuel consumption, even at cruising speed. She has substantial tankage, as befits a liveaboard, of 640 gallons of water and 620 gallons of fuel.

The 48' Packet version is a modified version of the 45' ferry design, with a pointed bow and a little different layout. She was intended to be built in steel, though she could be designed for plywood or aluminum also. Her styling is evocative of the coastal steamers of a couple generations ago, with a pleasantly salty look.

Like the 45, the 48 has room for lots of luxury touches, like the hot tub let in flush under the aft deck. Her layout has three private staterooms, each with a private head and shower stall. This is a layout that would be suited to both living aboard and use in charter work.

The 60' Schoolship is one of the oldest of our ferry designs. She is an idea we worked up in conjunction with a company that operated a charter boat out of Seattle. A large part of their work was taking out marine biology groups, and they thought they might be able to expand their work if they had a bigger boat that was set up to be a better working platform. They got caught up in budget cuts in the school districts, so we never got to try this one out.

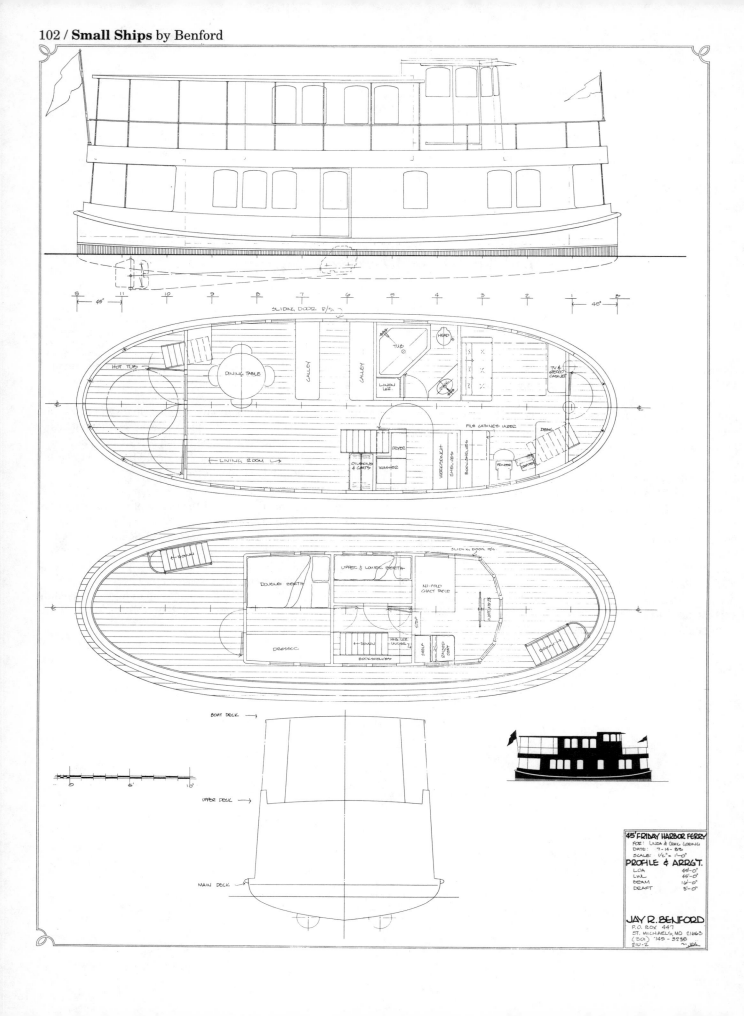

45' FRIDAY HARBOR FERRY
FOR: LINDA & CRAIG LORING
DATE: 7-14-83
SCALE: 1/2" = 1'-0"
PROFILE & ARR'G'T.
LOA   45'-0"
LWL   45'-0"
BEAM   16'-0"
DRAFT   3'-0"

JAY R. BENFORD
P.O. BOX 447
ST. MICHAELS, MD 21663
(301) 745-3235
210-2

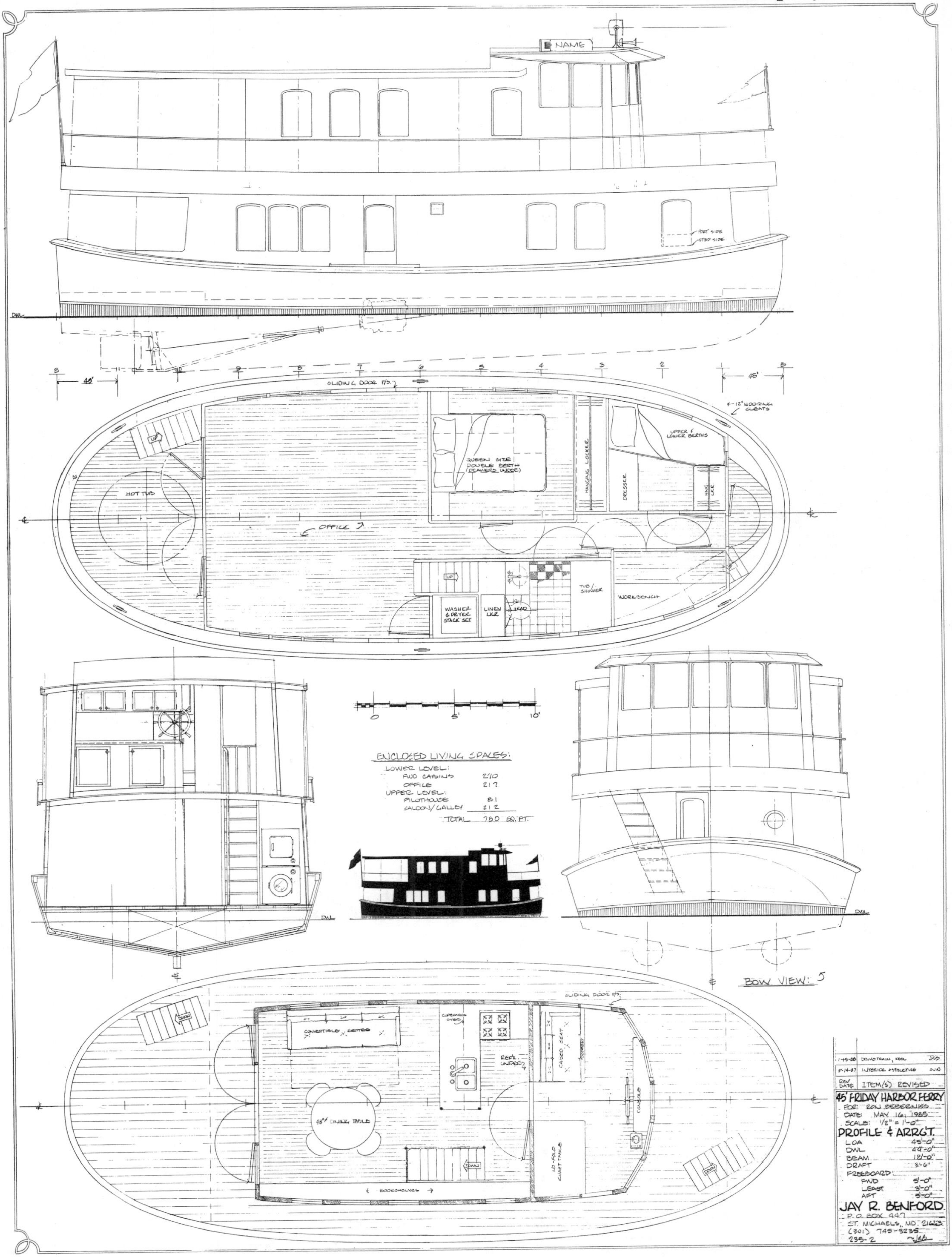

NAME

PORT SIDE
STBD SIDE

DWL

SLIDING DOOR P/S.

12" MOORING CLEATS

HOT TUB

QUEEN SIZE DOUBLE BERTH (DRAWERS UNDER)

HANGING LOCKER

DRESSER

UPPER & LOWER BERTHS

HANG LKR.

OFFICE

WASHER & DRYER STACK SET

LINEN LKR.

HEAD

TUB/SHOWER

WORKBENCH

ENCLOSED LIVING SPACES:
LOWER LEVEL:
  FWD CABINS   270
  OFFICE   217
UPPER LEVEL:
  PILOTHOUSE   81
  SALOON/GALLEY   212
    TOTAL   780 SQ. FT.

0   5'   10'

BOW VIEW: 5

CONVERTIBLE SETTEE

CUPBOARD OVER

STOWAGE

CABOOSE OVEN

REF. UNDER

CHAISE

SLIDING DOOR P/S.

48" DINING TABLE

4-FOLD GUEST TABLE

BOOKSHELVES

REV DATE	ITEM(S) REVISED	
1-13-88	DRIVETRAIN, KEEL	JRB
5-14-87	INTERIOR & STRUCTURE	JRB

45 FRIDAY HARBOR FERRY
FOR: RON BERBERIAN
DATE: MAY 16, 1985
SCALE: 1/2" = 1'-0"
PROFILE & ARRGT.
LOA   45'-0"
DWL   44'-0"
BEAM   18'-0"
DRAFT   3'-6"
FREEBOARD:
  FWD   5'-0"
  LEAST   3'-0"
  AFT   5'-0"

JAY R. BENFORD
P.O. BOX 447
ST. MICHAELS, MD. 21663
(301) 745-3235
235-2

PARTICULARS:

LOA   48'-0"
DWL   47'-6"
BEAM   13'-0"
DRAFT   4'-0"

48' COASTAL PACKET
FOR: MITTERNIGHT
1/4"= 1'-0"   9-25-87
OUTBOARD PROFILE

JAY R. BENFORD
P.O. BOX 447
ST. MICHAELS, MD. 21663
(301) 745-3235

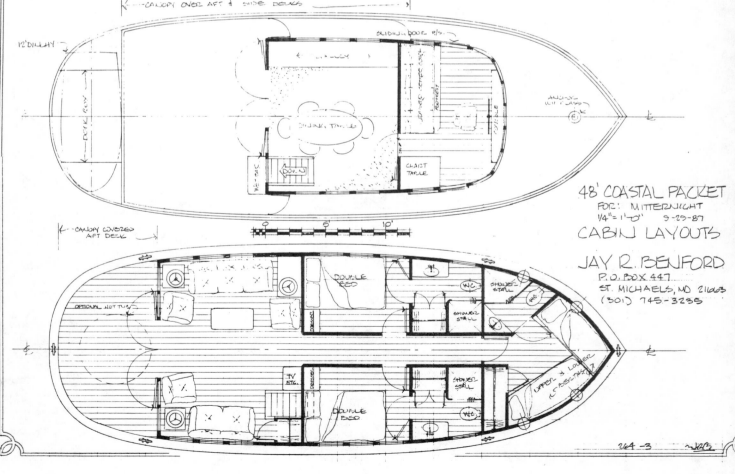

48' COASTAL PACKET
FOR: MITTERNIGHT
1/4"= 1'-0"   9-25-87
CABIN LAYOUTS

JAY R. BENFORD
P.O. BOX 447
ST. MICHAELS, MD. 21663
(301) 745-3235

264-3

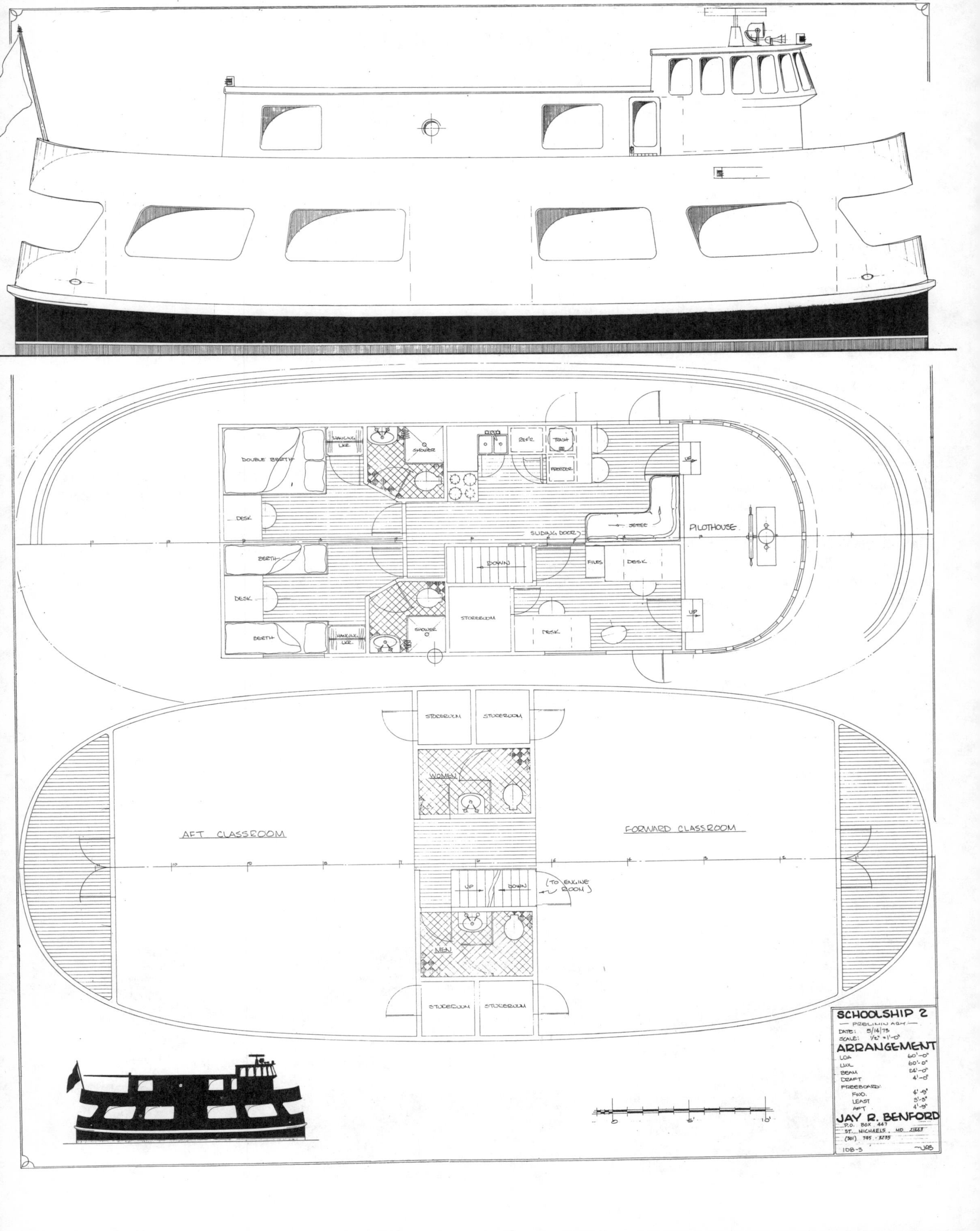

DOUBLE BERTH

HANGING LKR.

SHOWER

REFR.

TRASH

FREEZER

DESK

BERTH

SLIDING DOOR

SETTEE

PILOTHOUSE

DOWN

FILES

DESK

DESK

SHOWER

STOREROOM

UP

HANGING LKR.

BERTH

DESK

UP

STOREROOM

STOREROOM

WOMEN

AFT CLASSROOM

FORWARD CLASSROOM

UP

DOWN

(TO ENGINE ROOM)

MEN

STOREROOM

STOREROOM

SCHOOLSHIP 2
— PRELIMINARY —
DATE: 5/14/75
SCALE: 1/2" = 1'-0"
ARRANGEMENT

LOA	60'-0"
LWL	60'-0"
BEAM	24'-0"
DRAFT	4'-0"
FREEBOARD:	
FWD.	6'-9"
LEAST	3'-3"
AFT	4'-9"

JAY R. BENFORD
P.O. BOX 447
ST. MICHAELS, MD 21663
(301) 745-3235

10B-3

65' PATRIOT

The PATRIOT of St. Michaels is a new 65' excursion boat, now in service at St. Michaels, Maryland. Her primary services are scenic/historic river tours for up to 210 persons, and dinner cruises for about 90 persons. She replaces an older wooden vessel that Captain David P. Etzel, Jr., had operated on that service for a number of years.

The PATRIOT was designed by the Benford Design Group of St. Michaels, MD, specialists in small ships and cruising yachts. She was built of steel in Norfolk, VA. Her lower house has the heads, stairs, and service area all aft, with the rest of the house one wide-open space of about 940 square feet, making her very versatile in adapting to different service needs. She can be used for meal service, dances, weddings, live music groups, or small theater productions — all in a climate controlled space.

The upper deck features a classic round front pilothouse, with elevated bridge around it, for excellent visibility for the captain. There is abundant open air seating also, with a drink and snack service area just aft of the pilothouse.

The designers spent extra effort in creating a vessel that would almost double the prior boat's capacity, with 8' more beam (26' total), and still be driven a little faster; all with lowered fuel consumption and a reduced wake. She admeasures 50 gross tons, has fuel tankage for 2,400 gallons and water tankage for 1,300 gallons.

Captain Etzel and all the other captains and owners of the excursion boats that have been aboard the PATRIOT have remarked that in esthetics, practicality, and economy, "This is the best 65-footer I've ever seen!"

The following illustration shows one of the things we do as a part of designing a developable surface hull, whether for steel, aluminum, plywood, or fiberglass panels. It's part of the sophisticated computer design software we use, and allows us to "unwrap" the surfaces to a flat panel.

During the design process, we use it as a check against proposed materials sizes, whether it be 8' wide sheets of steel or plywood or some other size chosen by us or the builder. It's a real pain — let alone expense — for the builder to have to splice on a few extra inches in width to make up a panel. If we can design around the standard material sizes while it's easy to make changes either on paper or in the computer, it is a considerable savings for the builder, which can translate to profits to the builder and a reasonable price to the owner.

This process also is a help in the design work, allowing us to have accurate areas for doing weight calculations. Computers have certainly changed the way we do design work, and let us do more work in less time. This translates into better and more accurate design work and results in boats that perform better and can be built in less time.

Designs like the PATRIOT can be done in almost any size. Do you need a 50, 100, or 500 passenger excursion boat? This type of simple, yet elegant, working vessel can be a good basis for a boat that will produce good earnings. If you take our smaller ferry designs and add this sort of hull form you will have a good idea of what can be done in the smaller sizes.

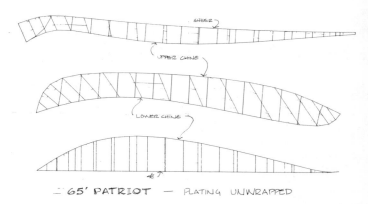

65' PATRIOT — PLATING UNWRAPPED

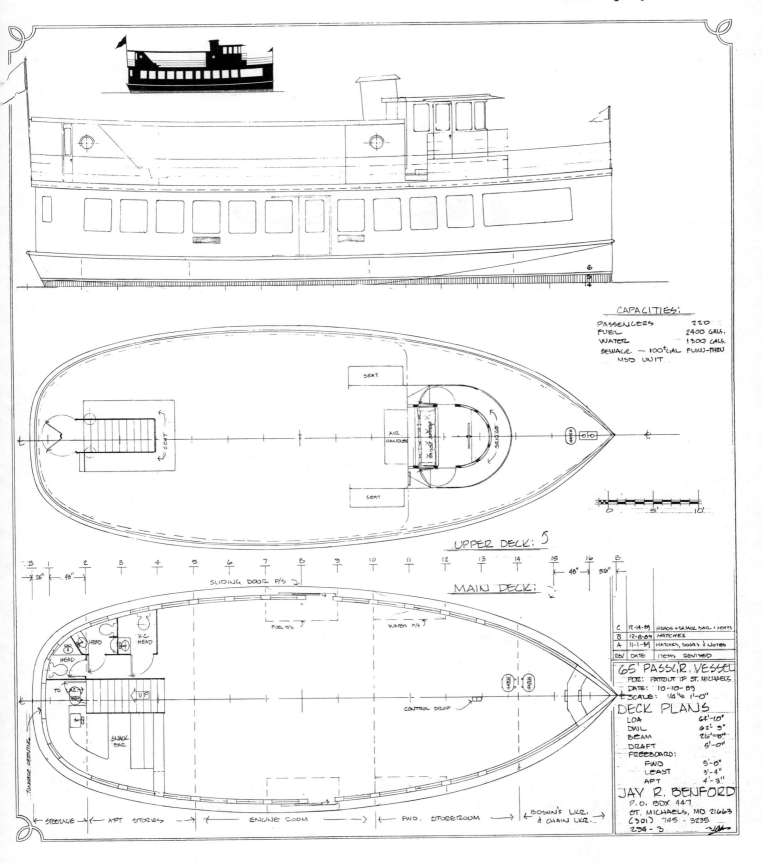

CAPACITIES:
PASSENGERS — 220
FUEL — 2400 GALS.
WATER — 1300 GALS.
SEWAGE — 100±GAL FLOW-THRU
MSD UNIT

UPPER DECK:

MAIN DECK:

C	12-14-89	HEADS + SNACK BAR + SEATS
B	12-8-89	HATCHES
A	11-1-89	HATCHES, DOORS & NOTES
REV	DATE	ITEMS REVISED

65' PASSGR. VESSEL
FOR: PATRIOT OF ST. MICHAELS
DATE: 10-10-89
SCALE: 1/4"= 1'-0"

DECK PLANS
LOA — 64'-10"
DWL — 62'-3"
BEAM — 20'-8"
DRAFT — 5'-0"
FREEBOARD:
FWD — 5'-0"
LEAST — 3'-4"
AFT — 4'-3"

JAY R. BENFORD
P.O. BOX 447
ST. MICHAELS, MD 21663
(301) 745-3235
234-3

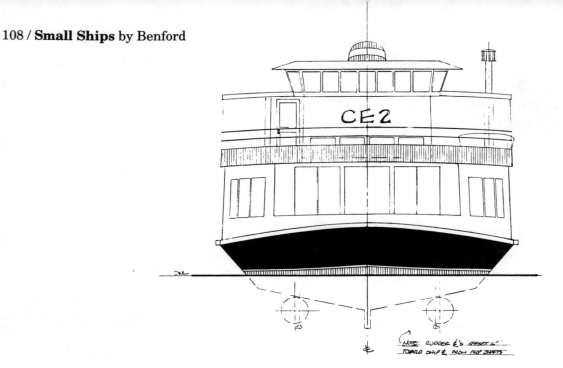

72' CE2

The brief for this design was for a boat to operate as a conference and entertainment (thus CE) facility for a waterfront hotel. With ever increasing demands on waterfront hotels for room capacity, this would let the usual space allocated for conference rooms be used for more bedrooms. Additionally, the boat would provide a feature that would attract groups to meet on it as a change of pace from the typical and mundane.

The people using the facility could thus have the choice of whether they wanted an uninterrupted day afloat, away from the demands of ringing phones with a continually changing vista. Or, they could stay tied to shore, to let the participants come and go during the meeting or party.

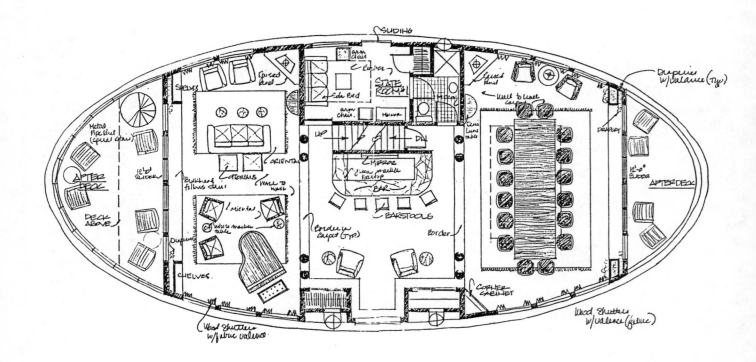

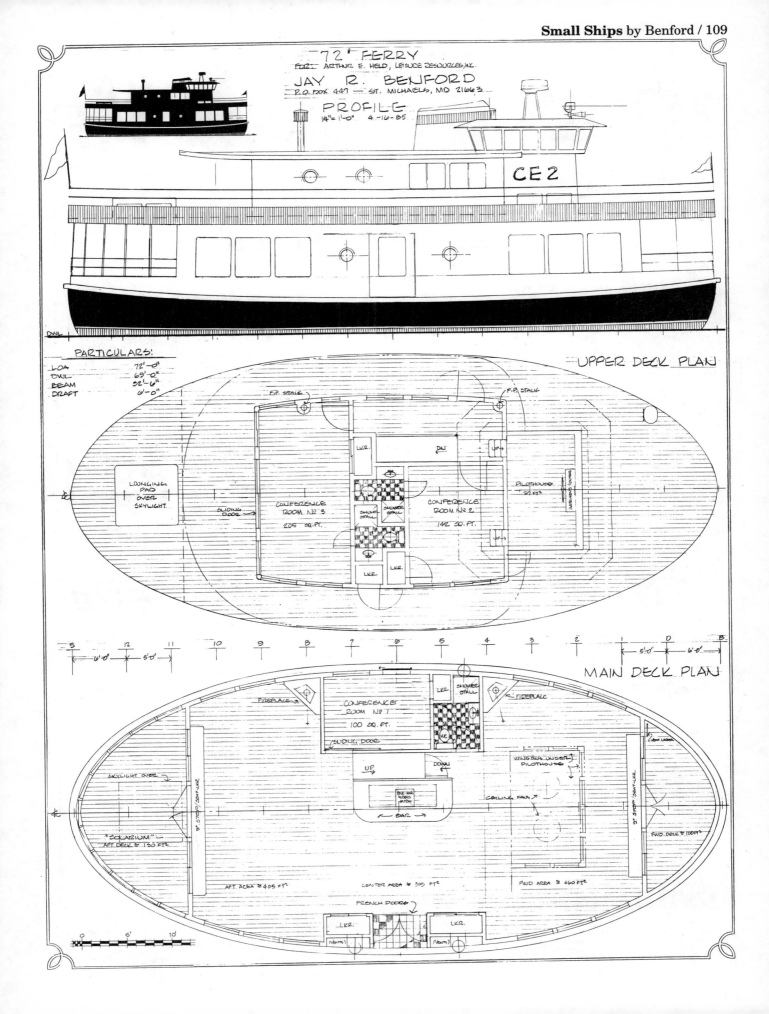

72' FERRY
FOR: ARTHUR E. HELD, LEISURE RESOURCES, INC.

JAY R. BENFORD
P.O. BOX 447 — ST. MICHAELS, MD 21663

PROFILE
1/4" = 1'-0"   4-16-85

CE 2

PARTICULARS:

LOA	72'-0"
DWL	69'-0"
BEAM	22'-6"
DRAFT	6'-0"

UPPER DECK PLAN

F.P. STALK

F.P. STALK

LOUNGING PAD OVER SKYLIGHT.

LKR.

SLIDING DOOR

CONFERENCE ROOM Nº 3
205 SQ. FT.

SHOWER STALL

SHOWER STALL

UP

CONFERENCE ROOM Nº 2
142 SQ. FT.

PILOTHOUSE
92 FT²

INSTRUMENT COVERS

UP

LKR.

LKR.

MAIN DECK PLAN

FIREPLACE

CONFERENCE ROOM Nº 1
100 SQ. FT.

LKR.

SHOWER STALL

W.C.

FIREPLACE

SLIDING DOOR

UP

DOWN

WINDOWS UNDER PILOTHOUSE

VENT LADDER

SKYLIGHT OVER

BAR

BOX STEP / SEAT-LIKE

ENG. RM. ACCESS HATCH

CEILING FANS

BOX STEP / SEAT-LIKE

"SOLARIUM"
AFT DECK ≅ 150 FT²

FWD. DECK ≅ 100 FT²

AFT AREA ≅ 405 FT²

CENTER AREA ≅ 315 FT²

FWD AREA ≅ 160 FT²

FRENCH DOORS

LKR.

LKR.

(VENTS)

(VENTS)

0   5'   10'

27' FLATTIE
27' x 24'2" x 8' x 2'
Plywood
Study plans $7

36' C.B. KETCH
36' x 28' x 11' x 2'6"/6'11"
Cold-molded
"Presto"/type/35' version
Study plans $11

36' CRUISER
36' 7½" x 35' x 13'6" x 3'6"
Plywood
39' version available
Study plans $11

35' TRAWLER YACHT STRUMPET
35' x 32' x 12'4½" x 4'6"
Carvel or cold-molded
Motorsailer version avail.
Study plans $11

34' SAILING DORY "BADGER"
34' x 28' x 11' x 4'6"
Plywood
Study plans $7

36' SAILING DORY "DONNA"
36' x 31' x 11' x 4'6"
Plywood or aluminum.
Study plans $7

CLASSIC BOAT PLANS

These distinctive boat designs are a selection from the board of **Jay R. Benford**, shown in his *Catalog Packet* ($10 postpaid) and his book *Cruising Yachts* ($35 postpaid). To order your own copies use the coupon below or write to:

P.O. Box 447–A, St. Michaels, MD 21663

32' TUG YACHT
32' x 30' x 13' x 3'
Steel
Other sizes available
Study plans $11

37' PILOTHOUSE CUTTER "CORCOVADO"
37' x 33' x 12'4" x 5'
Cold-molded or Carvel
3 rigs, 4 interiors
35' & 40' versions
Study plans $29

34' TOPSAIL KETCH "SUNRISE"
34'6" x 30'8" x 11'3" x 6'3"
Carvel
Alt. Great Pyramid rig
Study plans $15

20' FALSE CREEK FERRY
20' x 19' x 8' x 2'
Plywood
Many serving Expo 86
Study plans $7

14' TUG "GRIVIT"
14' x 13' x 7' x 3'
Cold-molded or Airex
Tug & Trawler yacht versions
Study plans $11

19' GUNKHOLER "CATSPAW"
19'6" x 18' x 7'9" x 1'4"/4'8"
Plywood
Study plans $7

This 38' Tug Yacht is one of over 100 Distinctive Benford Designs shown in our Catalog Packet. Send $10.00 for your own copy today.

20' SUPPLY BOAT "Baten"
20' x 19' x 7'11½" x 2'3"
Cold-molded, Carvel
or Airex
Study plans $7

20' TUG YACHT
20' x 18' x 8' x 2'3"
Airex (kits available)
Study plans $7

34' FRIDAY HARBOR FERRY
34' x 32'9" x 13'4" x 2'8"
Plywood
Great cruising liveaboard
Study plans $22

20' LAKE UNION CRUISER
20' x 19' x 7'11½" x 2'3"
Cold-molded, Carvel
or Airex
Study plans $7

18' TEXAS SKIFF
18' x 16' x 6'8½" x 5'
Batten seam
Study plans $7

17' CRUISER
17' 1½" x 16' x 7' x 2'
Cold-molded, Strip
or C-Flex
Study plans $7

17' FANTAIL STEAM LAUNCH
17' x 15'6" x 5'3" x 1'8"
Carvel, Strip or cold-molded
Study plans $7

30' TRAWLER YACHT "PETREL II"
30' x 27' x 11'3" x 3'6"
Carvel, Plywood or steel
Study plans $15

23' UTILITY BOAT
23' x 20' x 7'6" x 1'3"
Plywood/cold-molded
Study plans $7

45' FRIDAY HARBOR FERRY
45' x 44' x 18' x 3'9"
Plywood
Study plans $18.50

Why did *Cruising Sailboat Kinetics*, "a heavily illustrated showcase of the best cruising sailboat design of the last decade," include more designs by Jay Benford than any other designer? The author, Danny Greene, is the design editor of *Cruising World* magazine, and he gets to see all the best designs. He says, "Benford's boats all seem to have some sort of magical quality, a unique charater all their own that defies definition." And, "One often hears of a naval architect combining traditional design with modern building techniques. It may be that Jay Benford has created the ultimate marriage of the two in this breathtaking design."

You can learn more about these designs by reading *Cruising Yachts* by Jay R. Benford. It's filled with salty and practical solutions for your next cruising yacht. Use the order form and see for yourself. Only $35.00 postpaid, first class.

P.S. We Guarantee It!
If you're not satisfied that this is the greatest collection of innovative yacht designs you've seen, return the book within 15 days for a full refund.

44' FANTAIL MOTOR LAUNCH
44' x 40' x 12' x 3'
Cold-molded
Study plans $7

35' TUG YACHT
35' x 33' x 13'7½" x 4'
Cold-molded
Study plans $7

32' ST. PIERRE DORY "PROCTOR"
32' x 25'6" x 10'10½" x 2'8"
Plywood
Fishing /cargo hold
Study plans $11

34' FANTAIL CRUISER MEMORY
34' x 31' x 10'6" x 2'6"
Cold-molded
38' version available
Study plans $7

☐ Please send Benford's *Cruising Yachts* book and Catalog Packet for the special combination price of $40.

☐ I'm already enjoying my own copy of *Cruising Yachts*. Please just send the Catalog Packet for $10.

☐ Please send me the study plans of:

_____

_____

☐ Check or money order enclosed
☐ Please charge my VISA/MasterCard

Number _____

Exp. Date _____

Name _____
Address _____

Phone _____

JAY R. BENFORD
P.O. Box 447–A, St. Michaels, MD 21663
(301) 745–3235

**34' SAILING DORY
"BADGER"**
34' x 28' x 11' x 4' 6"
Plywood
Study plans $7

**34' SAILING DORY
"DONNA"**
36' x 31' x 11' x 4' 6"
Plywood
Study plans $7

20' FALSE CREEK FERRY
20' x 19' x 8' x 2'
Plywood
Many serving Expo 86
Study plans $7

**17' FANTAIL
STEAM LAUNCH**
17' x 15' 6" x 5' 3" x 1' 8"
Carvel, strip, or
cold-molded
Study plans $7

35' TUG YACHT
35' x 33' x 13' 7 1/2" x 4'
Cold-molded or Airex
Study plans $7

14' TUGBOAT
14' x 13' x 7' x 3'
Cold-molded or Airex
2 cruising versions
Study plans $11

**17' CRUISING CAT
"LIBERTY"**
17' x 15' 1 1/2" x 7' x 3' 6"
Strip-planked/cold-
molded, Airex or C-Flex
Sloop & yawl versions
Study plans $11

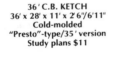

36' C.B. KETCH
36' x 28' x 11' x 2 6"/6'11"
Cold-molded
"Presto"-type/35' version
Study plans $11

**20' SUPPLY BOAT
BATEN**
20' x 19' x 7' 11 1/2" x 2' 3"
Cold-molded, Carvel, or
Airex
Study plans $7

20' TUG YACHT
20' x 18' x 8' x 2' 3"
Airex
Study plans $7

**18' CANOE YAWL
"IOTA"**
18' x 16' x 7' x 3'
Cold-molded
Study plans $7

**19' GUNKHOLER
"CATSPAW"**
19' 6" x 18' x 7' 9" x 1' 4"/4' 8"
Plywood
Study plans $7

CUSTOM DESIGNS

The creation of a first-class yacht takes more than just an excellent designer and builder. It also demands a client who has a clear vision of the vessel he wants and the persistence to keep refining the concept to be sure the details of the boat fit how he will use the boat.

With over 27 years of experience in designing distinctive boats, we've been privileged to work with quite a number of such clients. We usually have about a dozen projects "on the boards," with current projects ranging from 23' to 72'.

DESIGNS FOR PROFESSIONALS

Since 1962, working with a yard doing both stock 'glass and wood boats, we've been doing design work on production boats. In the time since, this has expanded to also include both steel and aluminum designs for professional builders.

For the builder looking to have a distinctive line of boats instead of clone-yachts, we'd be interested in talking. We find that a good design for a practical boat will create its own niche in the market and let you sell without major competition.

STOCK PLANS

Many of our previously done designs are available as stock plans. Our book *Cruising Yachts*, and our Catalog Packet will give a good overview of our prior work and an idea of the sorts of work that we can do.

THE IDEA FACTORY

One of the nice things about our design clientele is that we're not continually asked to do variations and clones of our previous designs. The infusion of fresh ideas from clients and builders with a variety of experiences is a critical part of this process.

If you have an idea you'd like to see brought to life, give us a call. Developing new ideas is our main business and what keeps us enthused and involved. We'll look forward to hearing from you.

For a better idea of the range and scope of the Benford Design Group's work, order their *Cruising Yachts* book ($35) and their Catalog Packet ($10) for a special combination price of $40.

**To order your own copies,
use the coupon here or call or write:**

JAY R. BENFORD
P.O. Box 447–A, St. Michaels, MD 21663
(301) 745-3235

50' D.E. KETCH
50' x 43' x 15' x 7'
Cold-molded, C-Flex,
Airex or Steel
Brigantine, cargo-hold
version
Study plans $22

**45' CUTTER
"ARGONAUTA"**
45' x 37' 6" x 12' 3" x 5'
Cold-molded or Steel
Study plans $15

**44' FANTAIL
MOTOR LAUNCH**
44' x 40' x 12' x 3'
Cold-molded
Study plans $7

**34' FANTAIL CRUISER
"MEMORY"**
34' x 31' x 10' 6" x 2' 6"
Cold-molded
38' version available
Study plans $7

39' CRUISER
39' x 35' x 14' x 3' 6"
Plywood
36' version available
Study plans $11

**35' TRAWLER YACHT
"STRUMPET"**
35' x 32' x 12' 14 1/2" x 4' 6"
Carvel or cold-molded
Motorsailer version
available
Study plans $11

14' CRUISER "HAPPY"
13' 10" x 13' 8" x 6' 3" x 3' 7"
Cold-molded
Study plans $11

30' SAILING DORY
30' x 26' x 10' x 4'
Plywood
Study plans $11

"The magical quality of Benford's Boats"

Why did *Cruising SailboatKinetics,* "a heavily illustrated showcase of the best cruising sailboat designs of the last decade," include more designs by Jay Benford than by any other designer? The author, Danny Greene, is the design editor of Cruising World magazine and he gets to see all the best designs. He says, "Benford's boats all seem to have some sort of magical quality, a unique character all their own that defies definition." And, "Few designers are more adept at imbuing their creations with such a charming touch as Benford." And, "The most impressive feature of the Benford 38 is its enormous innovative interior and deck/cabin arrangement. Benford has the ability to combine this with a salty and charming appearance. It is hard to imagine any designer fitting more accommodations into a 30-foot waterline boat without transforming the design into a Greyhound bus." And, "As always, Benford has cleverly designed the deck and cabin to combine good appearance, spaciousness below and ease of work on deck...She will surely attract attention and compliments in any anchorage." And, "...another impeccably drawn vessel from the board of Jay R. Benford..." And, "One often hears of a naval architect combining traditional design with modern building techniques. It may be that Jay Benford has created the ultimate marriage of the two in this breathtaking design."

You can learn more about these designs by reading *Cruising Yachts* by Jay R. Benford. It's filled with salty and practical solutions for your next cruising yacht.

P.S. We Guarantee It!
If you're not satisfied that this is the greatest collection of innovative yacht designs you've seen, return the book within 15 days for a full refund.

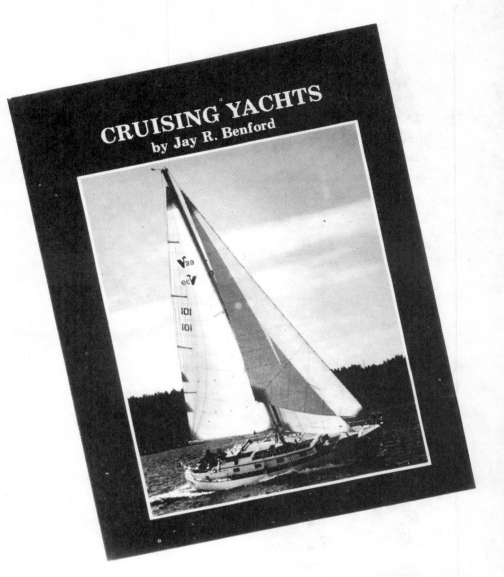

Jay Benford is one of those freethinking designers who is just as happy working on a 14 ft. (4.27m) worldgirdler as a 131 ft. (40m) luxury cruiser. His magic is such that he can make both boats, and all those in between, individual, attractive and practical.

Cruising Yachts...is distinguished...by the chapters on Benford designs; the pages of commonsense, on design and yacht building; theory and practice of cruising and even articles on the best time to go cruising and how to get the most from your money.
Dick Johnson
Yachting World

CRUISING YACHTS

by Jay R. Benford

Jay Benford is a widely known yacht designer with a far-ranging imagination and great versatility, unbound by prejudices on materials or methods of construction. This selection from his work covers both sail and power craft, from a 14-footer designed for a singlehanded circumnavigation to a 131' luxury yacht. Included are chapters on choosing a vessel, engines and horsepower, the custom design process, economy, rigs, and more. For the sailor looking for ideas, Benford is always interesting.
200 pp. Photos and study plans. $29.95

Wooden Boat

A broad selection of Benford's inimitable cruising designs, copiously illustrated with lines, plan, profile, construction, and detail drawings, and scores of fine photographs—many in full color. Each design is discussed in detail for its concept, construction, performance, and existing and possible variations (a Benford specialty), and the book also contains articles on yacht design aesthetics, the proper offshore yacht, designing for fuel economy, the custom design process, and more. Designs include the versatile Benford 30, fully illustrated in many of its variant forms; Benford's 30' to 37½' sailing dories, "the most economical offshore cruisers"; a number of distinguished and proven cruisers in the 30' to 45' range; a 14-footer designed for singlehanded circumnavigation; several versions of the "Friday Harbor Ferry", a stable, economical, cruising houseboat that Benford believes is the shape of waterfront living to come—and well may be; and a 131' cold-molded luxury cruising yacht designed and engineers for a Brasilian client. "Magical...a unique character all their own" writes Danny Greene of Benford's designs.

Waterlines